THE
REFERENCE
SHELF

HUMAN RIGHTS

edited by THOMAS DRAPER

THE REFERENCE SHELF

Volume 54 Number 1

THE H. W. WILSON COMPANY

New York   1982

THE REFERENCE SHELF

The books in this series contain reprints of articles, excerpts from books, and addresses on current issues and social trends in the United States and other countries. There are six separately bound numbers in each volume, all of which are generally published in the same calendar year. One number is a collection of recent speeches; each of the others is devoted to a single subject and gives background information and discussion from various points of view, concluding with a comprehensive bibliography. Books in the series may be purchased individually or on subscription.

Library of Congress Cataloging in Publication Data Card

Main entry under title:

Human Rights.
  (Reference staff ; v. 54, no. 1)
  Bibliography: p.
  1. Civil rights—Addresses, essays, lectures.
  2. United States—Foreign relations—1945–   —Addresses, essays, lectures.   I. Draper, Thomas.
  II. Series.
  JC571.H7684   341.4'81   81-22033
  ISBN 0-8242-0665-7   AACR2

PRINTED IN THE UNITED STATES OF AMERICA

CONTENTS

3

PREFACE

The history of mankind could also be described as the history of the long struggle to assert and then to protect human rights. The whole development of a concept of human rights is examined in this compilation. In search of religious and political freedom, Europeans left the Old World to settle the continent of North America where gradually they enacted guarantees of their liberties in documents as early as 1701—Pennsylvania's Charter of Privileges—and, later, the Declaration of Independence, the Constitution and its first ten amendments known as the Bill of Rights.

In our own century, Franklin D. Roosevelt set forth the Four Freedoms in a message to Congress: freedom of speech, freedom of worship, freedom from want, and freedom from fear. This was followed by the joint Anglo-American Atlantic Charter (1941) incorporating the Four Freedoms as well as promulgating for the first time both economic and social rights.

In the aftermath of World War II, it was President Harry S. Truman who declared that "A requisite for peace among nations is common respect for basic human rights." The founding of the United Nations in 1945 with the signing of the UN Charter marked the first agreement among nations to promote and observe "human rights and fundamental freedoms for all." The first definition of what actually was meant by "human rights" was not delineated until 1948 in the UN Universal Declaration of Human Rights.

Since then the Declaration has come to be regarded as basic international law, augmented later by the International Covenant on Civil and Political Rights and the International Covenant on Economic, Social and Cultural Rights. In addition, agreements on a regional basis have been established by the Western Hemisphere's Organization of American States

as well as the European Convention for the Protection of
Human Rights and Fundamental Freedoms.

In 1975, the Helsinki Final Act signed by the U.S., Canada, the Soviet Union, and 32 Eastern and Western European
nations, included a section on human rights calling for greater
freedom in the interchange of ideas and information and in
the movement of people between East and West.

Continuing American concern with assisting freedom
overseas was attested to by the action of Congress in 1975 establishing a Coordinator for Humanitarian Affairs in the Department of State and requiring that Department to publish
an annual survey on the status of human rights in all countries
receiving U.S. aid. In 1977 President Jimmy Carter used the
occasion of his inaugural address to state that "Our commitment to human rights must be absolute . . . Because we are
free we can never be indifferent to the fate of freedom elsewhere."

As the new Reagan Administration came into office in
1981, it appeared to embark on a course with human rights an
issue of low priority. Secretary of State Alexander Haig stated
that "International terrorism will take the place of human
rights in our concern, because it is the ultimate abuse of
human rights." Strong opposition in the Senate to the nomination of Ernest W. Lefever as Assistant Secretary of State for
Human Rights caused the White House to withdraw his name
in June and leave the position unfilled for several months before nominating Elliot Abrams to the post in October 1981.
Among several factors cited was Lefever's opposition to any
public criticism by the U.S. of human rights violations abroad,
particularly in right-wing regimes, and to publication of the
annual rights reports to Congress on individual countries.

In this volume many of the articles are concerned with
the question of how our foreign policy can not only reflect but
also demonstrate our belief in and adherence to individual
liberty—humans rights—without weakening U.S. security
and interests around the world.

The first section of articles reprinted here relates the
background and history of the human rights movement. The

second section attempts a brief international survey of human rights conditions today. Section III presents articles debating to what extent human rights should be an active factor in the making of U.S. foreign policy.

The editor wishes to thank the authors and publishers of the articles that follow for permission to reprint them in this compilation.

THOMAS DRAPER

November 1981

I. BACKGROUND AND HISTORY

EDITOR'S INTRODUCTION

The articles in this section present an overall view of the human rights movement. A historical perspective is given in the first article prepared by the editors of the Foreign Policy Association. "In the West, the individual comes first and the state helps assure the liberty that is his birthright. In Communist and other one-party states, the individual is subordinate to the state and is permitted only such rights as the state sees fit to grant."

Patricia Derian, the first U.S. Assistant Secretary of State for Human Rights (during the Carter Administration), espouses in the next selection "making human rights a central part of U.S. foreign policy," based on the "emerging, growing, and indeed, vigorous body of international law of human rights." At present, as the former Assistant Secretary points out: "The major flaw in the development of human rights law is one of enforcement . . . There is no formal international judicial system in which human rights laws are regularly adjudicated."

As the next selection shows, however, the very fact of the existence of these international covenants has "marked a fundamental change in nation-state relations: National sovereignty can no longer be a bar to international challenge to a government's denial of its citizens' rights."

The fourth selection is a proclamation by President Jimmy Carter commemorating the adoption of the UN Universal Declaration of Human Rights on December 10, 1948 and the U.S. Bill of Rights on December 15, 1791. By linking these two dates in a joint observation of Human Rights Week, the President highlighted America's concern not only for its own peoples' human rights but also for those of people all over the world.

The next article is an exhortation from a distinguished giant of the civil rights movement—the late Roger Baldwin, founder of the American Civil Liberties Union—on the need to assert these rights steadfastly or to risk losing them.

In the concluding article from the *New Yorker*, the focus is on certain attitudes towards both human and civil rights within the White House during the first months of the Reagan Administration.

FROM CAVE TO INTERNATIONAL COVENANT[1]

Freedom is the absence of force and the ability to do what one wishes—to eat and to work, to vote and to worship, to travel and to speak one's mind, to receive a fair and speedy trial. Freedom, writes Herbert J. Muller, author of *The Uses of the Past*, is "the condition of being able to choose and to carry out purposes."

The history of freedom begins with man's using his distinctive powers of the mind to meddle with the natural environment. By constructing irrigation and drainage systems, building cities, inventing writing and increasing his power over the environment, he also gained more effective freedom.

The first recorded use of a word meaning freedom goes back to the 24th century B.C. when the Sumerian king Urukagina of Lagash, the first known social reformer, put a stop to the abuse of his citizen-subjects by running the tax collectors out of town and curbing the excesses of the high priest.

Urukagina was well ahead of his time. Centuries passed before all-powerful rulers gave more than fleeting attention to their subjects' welfare. And then it was in the West—in the Greek city-states and in Rome—that the concept of civil and political rights of the individual took root. The legacy of ancient Athens was democracy—albeit a minority democracy of

[1] Excerpted from *Great Decisions '78*, a book by the Editors of the Foreign Policy Association. Foreign Policy Association. '78. p 5–14. © Copyright, 1978, Foreign Policy Association, Inc. Reprinted by permission.

slave-owning citizens. And the legacy of the Roman republic was the concept of citizens' rights under law.

The Greco-Roman models of democratic rights and individual freedoms were not lost, but many centuries were to pass before they were emulated by a handful of Western countries. In England the absolute power of the king was first curbed by the Magna Carta in 1215. As late as 1679, when the Habeas Corpus Act was signed, Englishmen were still subject to arbitrary arrest and indefinite imprisonment without trial. The original English Bill of Rights was only passed in 1689.

'Unalienable Rights'

At roughly the same time that the civil and political liberties of the individual were beginning to win recognition in the West, the concept of freedom itself was expanding. Out of the religious turmoil of the 16th century known as the Protestant Reformation emerged acceptance of the idea that the individual has freedom of conscience and the right of dissent. Such rights are not conferred by society or governments, asserted the 17th-century English philosopher John Locke and the 18th-century French philosopher Jean-Jacques Rousseau; they are rights with which the individual is born.

That revolutionary doctrine of natural rights is embodied in France's Declaration of the Rights of Man and of the Citizen (1789) and in our own Declaration of Independence: "We hold these Truths to be self-evident, that all Men are created equal, that they are endowed by their Creator with certain unalienable Rights . . ."

The U.S. Constitution separates and limits the government's power over the individual; the Bill of Rights (the first ten amendments to the Constitution) spells out his civil and political rights, including freedom of speech, press, religion, the right of assembly and the right to a speedy and public trial secured by an independent judiciary.

In the 19th century, a quite different and much older concept of freedom reappeared, especially in Europe. This was the right of whole peoples, united by language or culture or national identity, to be free from oppression by an alien ruler—the *collective* right of self-determination. The appeals of these nations and minorities for the right of self-determination hit a responsive chord because nationalism was by then a major political force. Some sympathetic governments even intervened militarily on behalf of such rebellious peoples, justifying their intervention on humanitarian grounds. In the 1820's, Greece, with outside help, fought for independence from the Ottoman Empire. Latin American republics freed themselves from the Spanish and Portuguese colonial yoke. The Balkan states of Rumania, Serbia and Montenegro rebelled and in 1899 gained their independence from Turkey. And the U.S. intervened to help Cuba free itself from Spanish misrule in 1898.

At the end of World War I the right of peoples to self-determination—one of President Woodrow Wilson's Fourteen Points—was widely accepted. But deciding what constitutes a "people" was not so easy. The victorious powers redrew Europe's boundaries and carved out a half-dozen new states— Estonia, Latvia, Lithuania and Poland from the old Russian empire; Czechoslovakia and Yugoslavia from what had been the greatest national hodgepodge of Europe, Austria-Hungary. The latter contained several nationalities, and rather than set up each nationality as independent, the League of Nations Covenant extended its protection to some 30 million national and linguistic minorities *within* the multinational states of Central and Eastern Europe. Meanwhile, far from European shores, the covenant also started another wave of self-determination by parceling out Germany's former colonies as "mandates" to the several Allied powers—and obligating the mandatories to *respect the rights* of the peoples under their tutelage.

With that one exception, the covenant contained no reference to human rights. Individual civil and political rights, not to mention economic and social rights, were not considered an appropriate concern of an international body; they were strictly the responsibility of governments.

It took a second world war to convince the international community that violations of individual human rights were a threat to the peace and that protection of those rights was a collective responsibility. The barbarous tyranny of Nazism and the extermination of 6 million Jews—and unnumbered people of other allegedly "inferior races"—demonstrated that deprivations of human rights go hand in hand with aggression.

At the same time, a further step was taken: the concept of human rights was extended to include not only civil and political rights but also economic rights. In listing their peace aims in the Atlantic Charter of August 1941, President Roosevelt and British Prime Minister Winston Churchill called for international collaboration to secure "for all, improved labor standards, economic advancement and social security . . ."— as well as the right of people to choose their own forms of government.

On the eve of victory in 1945, 50 nations with diverse political and economic systems met as United Nations founders in San Francisco. In ratifying the UN Charter, the members affirmed their faith in the dignity and worth of the individual and undertook an unprecedentedly broad obligation to promote universal respect for and observance of human rights and fundamental freedoms. Each nation pledged itself to work separately and in cooperation with the UN to implement its obligation.

The Charter does not define human rights. That task was left to future conferences. On December 10, 1948, the UN General Assembly adopted the Universal Declaration of Human Rights without a dissenting vote. (The Soviet bloc, Saudi Arabia and South Africa abstained.)

Universal Declaration of Human Rights

Whereas recognition of the inherent dignity and of the equal and inalienable rights of all members of the human family is the foundation of freedom, justice and peace in the world.

Whereas disregard and contempt for human rights have resulted in barbarous acts which have outraged the conscience of mankind, and the advent of a world in which

human beings shall enjoy freedom of speech and belief and
freedom from fear and want has been proclaimed as the highest aspiration of the common people, . . .

Now, therefore, The General Assembly

Proclaims THIS UNIVERSAL DECLARATION OF
HUMAN RIGHTS as a common standard of achievement for
all peoples and all nations . . .

All human beings are born free and equal in dignity and
rights. . . .

Everyone has the right to life, liberty and the security of
person.

No one shall be held in slavery or servitude . . .

No one shall be subjected to torture or to cruel, inhuman
or degrading treatment or punishment.

Everyone has the right to recognition everywhere as a
person before the law. . . .

No one shall be subjected to arbitrary arrest, detention or
exile.

—Adopted December 10, 1948

The declaration in time has come to be more than a mere
statement of basic principles. In the legislative work of the
UN it has become a standard of reference to which every new
text in human rights must conform. For new governments, it
has served as a model for their constitutions. And, according
to some experts, the declaration is now part of the customary
law of nations and therefore binding on all states, whether
they voted for it or not.

Not all lawyers agree on the last point. But there are international human rights treaties—called conventions or covenants—incorporating direct references to the declaration
that are binding on their signatories, in law if not in actual
practice. Principal among them are the two covenants which
were conceived as the first international bill of human rights:
the International Covenant on Civil and Political Rights, with
its Optional Protocol (nations which sign the protocol accept
the right of petition by individuals as well as by governments)
and the International Covenant on Economic, Social and Cultural Rights. The covenants were adopted by the General Assembly in 1966 and entered into force in 1976. The President

[Carter] signed them in October, but they have not been ratified. The Soviet Union is among the more than 40 signatories.

Two regional organizations have made significant contributions toward international observance of human rights. One is the Organization of American States (OAS), which adopted the American Declaration of the Rights and Duties of Man in Bogotá, Colombia, nine months before the UN approved the Universal Declaration. The other is the Council of Europe, a pioneer in developing machinery for the collective enforcement of human rights. Under the European Convention for the Protection of Human Rights and Fundamental Freedoms, adopted in 1950, an individual, group of individuals or nation whose rights have been violated can file a complaint with the European Commission of Human Rights. If a settlement isn't reached, the aggrieved party has recourse to the European Court of Human Rights or the Council of Europe's Committee of Ministers. All 19 Western European members of the council have ratified the convention. Indeed, respect for human rights is a condition for membership—and the condition is maintained. Portugal was not admitted until 1976, after democracy was established; and Spain is not yet a member.

The European commission served as model for the OAS Inter-American Commission on Human Rights, created in 1960. Its members are usually distinguished jurists of independent stature. The commission, which acts as a monitor of human rights in the Americas, has investigated violations in Cuba, Bolivia, Brazil, Chile, Haiti and elsewhere. In the last few years its effectiveness has been hurt by the refusal of some countries to permit on-the-spot investigations and pressures to curtail its activities.

Helsinki

A new chapter in the unfolding history of human rights was started in Helsinki, Finland, on August 1, 1975 when the U.S., Canada, the Soviet Union and 32 nations of Western and Eastern Europe signed the Final Act of the Conference on Security and Cooperation in Europe. In exchange for accepting as permanent the post-World War II map of Europe—Moscow's basic aim in originating the conference—the Western conferees obtained inclusion of a section known informally as Basket 3. The section calls for the freer movement of people, ideas and information between East and West. The act is a political statement of intent—not a treaty or legally binding agreement—but its modest undertakings on human rights have already had a powerful psychological influence in all the signatory countries.

It was left for a follow-up conference in 1977 to measure the extent of each country's implementation of the Helsinki acts' provisions. The U.S., in a mid-1977 report to the follow-up conference, charged that the Soviet Union and its allies "have advanced arguments and interpretations which seek to blunt the purpose of Basket 3 through token and selective implementation of its provisions." The August 1977 report of a joint congressional commission was even more critical. It declared that the Soviet Union had "shown systematic disregard for civil and political rights.". . . Like the act itself, resolutions adopted by the meeting will not be binding. But binding or not, Helsinki and Belgrade have focused attention on what the Kremlin insists are domestic matters—the widespread violations of human rights in its own country and in Eastern Europe.

Freedom Under Fire

International concern for human rights has come a long way in a short time. Thirty-odd years ago there were no internationally agreed standards of human rights or government behavior with respect to those rights; no international forum for discussing the subject; no procedures for investigating complaints; no continuing studies of particular rights and their violation. Today all those things exist—yet human rights advocates believe most of the hard part—implementation—lies ahead. Many would agree with Ambassador William W. Scranton, who told the UN in 1976, "Today the only universality that one can honestly associate with the Universal Declaration of Human Rights is universal lip service."

Few nations measure up to the declaration's "common standard of achievement." Moreover, there are basic disagreements—over the relative importance of the rights of the individual vs. the rights of society; over economic and social rights vs. civil and political rights. In the West, the individual comes first and the state helps assure the liberty that is his birthright. In Communist and other one-party states, the individual is subordinate to the state and is permitted only such rights as the state sees fit to grant.

Many developing countries' leaders insist that for them political rights are frills. What use, they ask, is freedom of speech to a starving man? Civil libertarians turn the question around: How can the starving man hope to improve his lot unless he can change the government that permits him to continue starving?

Three Basic Options

. . . What place should we make in our foreign policy for the ideals of freedom on which this nation was founded?

A case can be made for any of three broad options.

1. The idealistic option calls on our country to give top priority to human rights in our foreign policy, supporting that cause consistently and vigorously wherever people are not free—even if this means confrontations. To this end we should use all effective means short of war. These include public and diplomatic pressure, plus the leverage of withholding various benefits such as diplomatic relations, economic aid, trading privileges and other forms of cooperation. We should also bring to bear the force of international law and other standards of conduct, not only by joining and invoking existing treaties such as the International Covenant on Civil and Political Rights, but by working to build new and more enforceable world law to bring human rights violators to justice. And where deprivation of *economic* rights is a main obstacle to freedom, as in most of the third world, we should attack the roots of poverty by insisting on fundamental political and social reform as a condition of our aid.

Such a policy, its advocates would argue, will:

☐ promote a national foreign policy consensus reflecting our country's fundamental values—a policy the people can be proud of and be willing to sacrifice for.
☐ demonstrate to the world that America stands for something better than sheer power, something that responds to universal human aspirations.
☐ free our country from morally distasteful alliances with dictators.
☐ speed the evolution of a world community of freedom, the only kind of world in which our people can feel secure—since freedom is indivisible.

As [former] Secretary [of State Cyrus] Vance himself has said: "Our own well-being, and even our security, are enhanced in a world that shares common freedoms and in which prosperity and economic justice create the conditions for peace. . . . We always risk paying a serious price when we become identified with repression."

Proponents of this course reject the view that U.S. opposition to injustice in powerful countries, especially the Soviet Union, endangers our own interests in arms control and other East-West agreements. The Soviets, they argue, have as much interest in such accords as we have. Moreover, the Soviet Union itself pursues revolutionary goals around the world—in Angola, for example—and is free to advocate its beliefs in our own open society. Why should we shrink from pursuing our beliefs with the same vigor? As for warnings of a tinderbox in Eastern Europe, it is not our responsibility to help the Soviets police their empire; rather, we can help by peaceful means to keep alive a potential for autonomy in that area.

As for the problem of poverty and freedom, this view holds that third world economic development and political development are inseparable. We should not fear to press for land reform, equitable taxes, etc., even if this risks social turmoil, for the longer reform is postponed, the worse the turmoil will eventually be.

2. The security option calls for this country frankly to subordinate its ideal of universal freedom to the necessity to maintain and stabilize the global power balance with our

main adversary, the Soviet Union. In this perspective, the only freedom which we have a duty to promote and defend is the freedom of the American people. Abroad, the promotion of human rights is one of many U.S. foreign policy concerns, but in the thermonuclear age it ranks nowhere near the top. The primary consideration, as Senator John Sparkman (D-Ala.), [then] chairman of the Foreign Relations Committee, has said, "must remain the security of the U.S., its allies and its friends." This strategy does not mean an all-out arms race but rather a high priority for regulating the military and political competition with the Soviet Union—for unless that is done, grimly observes Sovietologist Marshall D. Shulman, "there will be no opportunity for the strengthening of democratic values."

According to this policy view, the U.S. should judge other governments only by how they deal with this country, not by how they treat their own people. Many a time we have felt the need to form relationships with dictators or oppressors in order to obtain some facility or geographic position, or to fill a strategic or economic need in our contest of power with the only country that can destroy us, the Soviet Union. We should never hesitate to do this. We should maintain diplomatic relations with any regime that controls a country and can protect Americans' interests there. We should give up our futile and quixotic passion for ridding the world of injustice. "Moral indignation," said the English historian Herbert Butterfield, "corrupts the agent who possesses it and is not calculated to reform the man who is the object of it." It is enough if we contribute to the universal cause of human rights by keeping a free America secure, and by promoting a more just society at home as an example to the world.

3. The pragmatic option holds that our foreign policy should avoid any rigid strategy or set of rules concerning human rights, but should treat each case as unique—balancing our security needs against human rights and other traditional ethical values.

This approach, while fully accepting our historic commitment to freedom, insists that we must responsibly recognize the limits of this or any other nation's capacity to shape world events. Like a prudent pensioner, we must learn not to live beyond our means, not to attempt more than we can perform. This is especially true in dealing with such a complex value as freedom, which cannot be imposed from the outside or conveyed as a gift, but must be earned and kept by the virtue and exertions of the peoples who seek it.

In pursuing human rights goals, this argument insists, perfectionism and cynicism are equal and opposite dangers. As the Carter Administration has acknowledged, we have security and economic interests which often call for dealings with undemocratic governments such as those in South Korea, Iran and South Africa, and such situations will continue to arise. Furthermore, societies which have little tradition of democracy may take many years of trial and error before they can deal with the stresses of free debate. They should not in the meanwhile be deprived of the aid and friendship of the U.S.

Moreover, denying aid or other benefits to all countries that violate human rights would mean punishing many countries that give important support to our other foreign policy goals.

Therefore, in determining its policy toward human rights violators, the U.S should study each unique case to determine the most appropriate response in the light of all our interests, human rights included. It should examine the extent of the violations: are they increasing or declining? It should consider the means for effective action as well as the possible undesired side effects. If aid to an oppressive government is withheld, for example, will we punish the victims along with their oppressors?

HUMAN RIGHTS AND INTERNATIONAL LAW[2]

It is rare in government to find that one's work immerses one in ideas and concepts which, over time, can have a pro-

[2] Reprint of statement by Assistant Secretary for Human Rights and Humanitarian Affairs, Patricia M. Derian, before the National Association of Women Judges, Washington, DC, October 3, 1980. Department of State Bulletin. United States. Department of State. Washington, DC 20520. Ja. '81. p 21–3.

found and lasting impact on the course of our country's future. But that has been my lot for the past 3½ years as I and others have sought to integrate the international concern for human rights into our relations and policies with other nations.

That effort—making human rights a central part of U.S. foreign policy—is perhaps the most innovative approach that the United States has ever taken in this area. It is an attempt to express our commitment to the protection and enhancement of human dignity throughout the world. It is a reflection of the values and traditions that have long been the hallmark of our country. With human rights as a major component of our foreign policy, the United States has made a sustained commitment to a world free from governmental violations of the integrity of the person; a world free from want of food, shelter, health care, and education; a world free to enjoy civil and political liberties.

While the philosophical content of our human rights policy may seem largely ethical, ideological, or political, what is often poorly understood is the major role that law has played in establishing a framework in which human rights and human decency can be promoted and furthered.

I have noted with some curiosity that, over the past few years, many people who should know better have been surprised to learn that there is an emerging, growing, and, indeed, vigorous body of international law of human rights. This lack of awareness may well be explained by the fact that there is no formal international judicial system in which human rights laws are regularly adjudicated. The lack of such a system has made difficult a general apprehension that international human rights law imposes substantial obligations on all governments.

Multilateral Treaties

While human rights law has not had the advantage of such a judicial system, which would aid in the development of a cohesive and coherent body of law, a law of human rights has, nonetheless, developed. Broadly, it has emerged as a result of international treaties; international customary law and practice; and domestic laws, regulations, and court decisions evidencing international custom or acceptance of general principles.

Of these, among the most important are the U.N. Charter and numerous international treaties and other instruments developed in an effort to promote respect for human rights.

The U.N Charter is probably the first and certainly the most important treaty to recognize human rights and fundamental freedoms of individual human beings as matters of legitimate concern to the entire world community. As set forth in Article 1 (3) of the charter, the purpose of the United Nations, among other things, is "to achieve international co-operation in solving international problems of an economic, social, cultural, or humanitarian character, and in promoting and encouraging respect for human rights and for fundamental freedoms for all without distinction as to race, sex, language, or religion." Article 55 states that the United Nations shall promote "universal respect for, and observance of, human rights and fundamental freedoms for all without distinction as to race, sex, language, or religion," while under Article 56 "all Members pledge themselves to take joint and separate action in co-operation with the [United Nations] for the achievement of the purposes set forth in Article 55."

Shortly after the founding of the United Nations, the idea of an international bill of human rights was advanced. The first step was taken on December 10, 1948, when the U.N. General Assembly adopted and proclaimed the Universal Declaration of Human Rights. The purpose of the declaration is to be ". . . a common standard of achievement for all peoples and all nations, to the end that every individual and every organ of society, keeping this Declaration constantly in mind, shall strive by teaching and education to promote respect for these rights and freedoms. . . ."

While adopted by the U.N. General Assembly, the declaration lacks the binding force of a treaty. It has, nonetheless, proved to be a frequently invoked explanation of the scope of the human rights and fundamental freedoms recognized by treaty—that is, by the U.N. Charter. It has also been contributing year by year to the development of a customary international law of human rights.

After adopting the declaration, the United Nations drafted, adopted, and opened for signature two major international covenants on human rights—one covering civil and political rights with an optional protocol; the other economic, social, and cultural rights. These three instruments complete the international bill of human rights begun with the Universal Declaration, providing legal as well as moral force to international human rights . . .

The charter and the two covenants are by no means the only multilateral effort at promoting human rights. There are over 20 treaties now in place and they include, *inter alia:* the Convention on the Prevention and Punishment of the Crime of Genocide, the International Convention on the Elimination of All Forms of Racial Discrimination, the Convention concerning the Abolition of Forced Labor, the American Convention on Human Rights, the Convention Relating to the Status of Refugees, the Convention on the Reduction of Statelessness, and numerous treaties for the promotion and advancement of women. Of these there are the Convention on the Political Rights of Women, the Convention on the Nationality of Married Women, and the recent Convention on the Elimination of All Forms of Discrimination Against Women, which the United States signed in Copenhagen this past summer. All of these conventions create binding legal obligations on the parties to them . . .

Regional Arrangements

It is not only on the global level that efforts to promote human rights take place; by and large, some of the most innovative attempts have occurred on regional levels. Indeed, it may well be that regional arrangements will most rapidly advance the commitment to human rights by all nations.

Perhaps the most highly developed regional achievement is the European Convention for the Protection of Human Rights and Fundamental Freedoms. The European convention established a commission and a court for handling both state and individual complaints. The members of the Organization of American States have promulgated the American Convention on Human Rights, which also includes both a commission and a court. Thus, for the first time in our history, a human rights court has been established in the Americas, headquartered in San Jose, Costa Rica. The League of Arab States has set up a Permanent Arab Commission on Human Rights. The Organization of African Unity is reviewing a draft on an African charter on human rights and the possibility of establishing a commission on human rights for Africa. Under the Helsinki Final Act of 1975, Western Europe, the United States, Canada, and Eastern Europe—35 nations—agreed upon a set of principles to reduce tension and political conflicts in Europe, including among them "respect for human rights and fundamental freedoms." With the exception of the Helsinki Final Act, which was made expressly nonbinding, each of these regional initiatives creates or contemplates creating legal obligations.

In some instances individuals are able to assert their human rights in courts or other appropriate forums. For example, the European Convention on Human Rights and the Optional Protocol to the Covenant on Civil and Political Rights establish specific procedures for the bringing of complaints by private individuals where the nation concerned has agreed to such a procedure. So, too, does the racial discrimination convention and the American Convention on Human Rights.

Role of Domestic Courts

Again internationally recognized human rights may be adjudicated by domestic courts in some jurisdictions. A case in point is the recent Pena case which was initially heard in the U.S. Eastern District Court of New York. The case involved a tort claim brought by the father and sister of a teenage Paraguayan who was allegedly tortured to death in Asuncion by the defendant Pena-Irala, a Paraguayan police officer who was found and served in New York. The suit was brought pursuant to a 1789 law, now codified as 28 U.S.C. section 1350. Section 1350 allows an alien to sue in Federal District Courts for a tort in violation of the law of nations or treaties of the United States.

Thus a threshold question confronting the court was whether torture is a violation of the law of nations in the sense of section 1350. If not, the court would lack jurisdiction to hear the case.

The district court considered itself bound, by views in earlier cases decided by the Second Circuit Court of Appeals, to reject jurisdiction. Those views appeared to exclude from the reach of the law of nations wrongs inflicted by a state on its own nationals.

On appeal, the second circuit sought an opinion from the State Department. The State Department drafted, and the Department of Justice filed, a brief showing that the international law of human rights today may extend to a wrong by a state against its own citizens and that torture is such a universally recognized wrong. The court of appeals adopted this view and remanded the case to the district court.

Some international treaties, such as the Genocide Convention, provide for the prosecution of individuals who have allegedly violated the human rights of others.

Frequently, the provisions of a particular human rights treaty are incorporated into the domestic law of a state in such a manner that it can be invoked directly by individuals. In some states, once a treaty is ratified, it automatically becomes a part of the domestic law; in others, additional implementing legislation is required. Needless to say, these are not merely academic concerns. Domestic courts in the United States are, at times, faced with the question of whether a human rights treaty is self-executing, thus permitting the benefits of the treaty to be applied directly to a litigant. I should note that in transmitting four human rights treaties to the Senate in February 1978, President Carter recommended that the United States declare that they are not self-executing.

During the early 1970s numerous suits were brought in domestic courts in an effort to "prevent the U.S. Government and other U.S. interests from aiding the forces of racial repression in southern Africa." While the suits did not succeed, they were of the utmost importance in raising the consciousness of lawyers, judges, government officials, and the general public to the existence of human rights law and its potential application in domestic courts.

While there is, in my view, a clearly recognizable code of human rights law binding on states and applicable to individuals, the major flaw in the development of human rights law in one of enforcement. The implementation of human rights law largely depends on the consent of nations. The competence of various international courts to render a judgment against a nation which has violated its human rights obligations rests on that nation's consent to the court's jurisdiction. However, even if that consent is forthcoming, an adverse judgment against a consenting nation may or may not be effectively enforced. Where a court may, as is the case of the International Court of Justice, render advisory opinions, those opinions, while deserving great respect, are, by definition, not binding, unless by virtue of some special agreement.

Currently, the implementation and enforcement of human rights law are largely dependent on voluntary compliance, moral pressures, and other forms of influence. Ideally, and perhaps with time, there will emerge a viable court system with the International Court of Justice as the final court of appeal. Already many of the regional arrangements for the promotion and protection of human rights have established some form of juridical mechanism for lodging complaints.

What I have sought to do here today is to show in a rather brief form that human rights is something more than a controversial, ideological, or political concept. Human rights is law and, as such, when a nation violates individual human rights, it is violating international law. The efforts of the U.S. Government to make human rights a central part of our foreign policy is, in effect, an effort to incorporate within our foreign policy the international law which establishes standards of human decency and human dignity. In that human rights is something beyond an ethical, ideological, or political concept and is also very much a legal concept.

The question I am often asked is: "What is the future of the U.S. human rights policy under a different Administration?" I say that if human rights is international law, and I believe that it is, there can be no other course for the U.S. Government but to apply and enforce that law.

What I have attempted to do here today is to provide a better understanding of the role that the law plays in enhancing human rights. The concept of human rights is a concept of world order. It is a proposal for structuring the world so that every individual's human worth is realized, every individual's human dignity is protected. The purpose of laws is to create a meaningful, rational, and just framework in which the pursuit of personal and societal enjoyment can take place. This thought has never been expressed better than in the preamble to the Universal Declaration of Human Rights. The drafters of the declaration clearly understood the important role that law must play if the goal of respect for universal human rights is ever to be realized. They wrote:

. . . it is essential, if man is not to be compelled to have recourse, as a last resort, to rebellion against tyranny and oppression, that human rights should be protected by the rule of law.

HUMAN RIGHTS AND U.S. FOREIGN POLICY[3]

The idea of human rights is almost as old as its ancient enemy, despotism. The first known use of a word meaning freedom was in the 24th century, BC, when a Sumerian king rid his people of an oppressive high priest.

[3] Reprinted from Department of State publication 8959. United States. Department of State. Bureau of Public Affairs. Office of Public Communication. Washington, DC 20520. D. '78. p 1–20.

But for centuries, omnipotent god-kings and emperors gave little thought to their subjects' welfare, and even ancient law codes did not mark out any areas of individual freedom from state control. It was another 2,000 years before the concept of civil and political rights of the individual really took root—in the city-states of Greece and the Athenian democratic experiments.

When Sophocles' heroine Antigone cries out to the autocratic King Creon:

> All your strength is weakness itself against
> The immortal unrecorded laws of God

she makes a deeply revolutionary assertion. There are laws, she claims, higher than the laws made by any king; as an individual she has certain rights under those higher laws; and kings and armies—while they may violate her rights by force—can never cancel them or take them away.

Sophocles wrote his play in 442 BC, but Antigone's brave cry has resounded through the ages. In Paris during World War II, at a revival staged as a disguised protest against the Nazi occupation, Frenchmen stood and cheered her words.

Athenian democracy, flawed though it was by slavery, was a priceless heritage. Later the Romans added their concepts of the rights of a citizen under the law and a single law for all peoples. These ideals, however, were submerged for centuries by the fall of Rome and the onset of the Dark Ages.

In medieval Europe, the first codifications of human rights began to emerge in compacts between kings and feudal lords. The most influential of these was the English Magna Carta, accepted by King John in 1215. Though it was exacted by his barons in their own special interests, several of its provisions gave strong expression to the idea of individual freedom for all men. Such was the famous Clause 39: "No freeman should be taken or imprisoned . . . or exiled or in any way destroyed . . . except by the lawful judgment of his peers or (and) the law of the land."

Centuries of struggle still lay ahead: As late as 1679, when the Habeas Corpus Act was signed, Englishmen could be kept in prison indefinitely without trial. But the 17th century saw the foundations of English liberty at last firmly laid in the Petition of Right (1628) and especially the English Bill of Rights (1689). The ideas and the words of these documents quickly found their way across the Atlantic to the New World colonies.

Meanwhile, the idea of freedom itself was growing broader. The individual's freedom of conscience and his right of dissent are not bestowed by governments, proclaimed the powerful philosophers of the Enlightenment, John Locke and Jean-Jacques Rousseau; they are rights with which the individual is born. And they are inalienable rights, the philosophers said, because they spring from a law of nature—a law in the light of which all individuals are born equal.

These ideas, too, found their way across the Atlantic.

American Involvement

Because so many of our early colonists were refugees from European persecution, the American colonies were fertile soil for the ideals of human rights. As early as 1641 the Massachusetts Body of Liberties provided that:

No man's life shall be taken away, no man's honor or good name shall be stayned, no man's person shall be arrested . . . no man's goods or estate shall be taken away from him . . . unlesse it be by vertue or cquitie of some expresse law of the country . . .

In 1644 Roger Williams guaranteed religious freedom to the settlers of Providence. In 1701 William Penn granted the Charter of Privileges to Pennsylvania—including full legal protection for the accused and safety of property except by due process of law. These strands of the American commitment to rights through law, reinforced by the ideas of the European Enlightenment, were woven together in the Declaration of Independence, the Constitution, and its first 10 amendments, the Bill of Rights.

These documents became the wellspring of America's legal and ethical concern with human rights. And their influence was not confined to America; reverberating across the Atlantic, they inspired the authors of the French Declaration of the Rights of Man and the Citizen (1789). Just as the French philosophers had helped to give the colonies an ideology, the revolution in the colonies in turn gave France an example to follow. Eventually, the example set by both the United States and France in adopting written constitutional guarantees of individual liberties was followed in much of the rest of the world.

Throughout the 19th century and into the 20th, the rights of Americans were continually redefined and expanded. The aftermath of the Civil War brought an end to slavery and assured, at least in theory, the right of every adult male to vote. In 1920 the franchise was extended to women as well.

In 1787, Thomas Jefferson wrote to James Madison that "a bill of rights is what the people are entitled to against every government on earth." In the 19th century, American Presidents expressed strong views against Czarist oppression of the Jews. The massacre of the Armenians under the Ottoman Empire drew Woodrow Wilson's condemnation, and the rhetoric of Wilson's call to Congress to declare war on the Central Powers was that "the world must be made safe for democracy." Shortly before America entered World War II, President Roosevelt gave the nation's commitment to human rights for all peoples a ringing new formulation as the Four Freedoms—freedom for speech and expression, freedom of worship, freedom from want, and freedom from fear.

Roosevelt's third freedom reflected further growth in the human rights concept: It had gradually come to encompass not only the traditional civil and political rights but economic and social rights as well. First popularized by socialist thinkers, these eventually won universal acceptance. In the Atlantic Charter of August 1941, Roosevelt and Churchill called for international cooperation to secure "for all, improved labor standards, economic advancement and social security."

The horrors of World War II, particularly the slaughter of six million Jews by the Nazis, convinced the international community that protection of human rights was a collective responsibility. "A requisite for peace among nations," as President Truman put [it] in 1947, "is common respect for basic human rights." And the United States took the lead in the effort to build, through the United Nations, a structure to promote human rights worldwide.

In signing the U.N. Charter, at San Francisco in 1945, all U.N. members reaffirmed their "faith in fundamental human rights, in the dignity and worth of the human person, in the equal rights of men and women and of nations large and small ..." They undertook an unprecedented obligation to promote "universal respect for, and observance of, human rights and fundamental freedoms for all without distinction as to race, sex, language, or religion." Each nation pledged itself to work separately and in cooperation with the United Nations to achieve these purposes.

The Charter did not define human rights. That task fell to a commission chaired by Eleanor Roosevelt. On December 10, 1948, the U.N. General Assembly approved the fruit of the commission's labors—the Universal Declaration on Human Rights. This was later supplemented by major human rights treaties, called conventions or covenants, and most recently by the Final Act of the Conference on Security and Cooperation in Europe, known as the Helsinki Final Act. These documents have marked a fundamental change in nation-state relations: National sovereignty can no longer be a bar to international challenge to a government's denial of its citizens' rights.

The dynamism of the early postwar years was not sustained in the 1950's, however, and in the 1960's the United States became increasingly preoccupied with its own civil rights movement and its deepening involvement in Vietnam.

Disillusionment over Vietnam, and a feeling that U.S. foreign policy had become too concerned with a narrow definition of security at the expense of moral values, led in the 1970's to a new and more assertive mood in Congress. A growing majority felt the American people would not support a foreign policy out of tune with national values, and opposed giving U.S. aid and arms to regimes that oppressed their citizens. In 1974 Congress voted to cut off security assistance to governments implicated in "a consistent pattern of gross violations" of human rights. It passed the Jackson-Vanik Amendment, tying trade benefits for the Soviet Union to a more liberal Soviet emigration policy (a linkage rejected by the U.S.S.R.). It broadened the limitation on security assistance to include economic and development aid. In 1976, it put restrictions on arms sales to human rights violators.

Congress also pushed for greater attention to human rights in the Department of State. A Coordinator for Human Rights and Humanitarian Affairs was appointed in 1976, and the Secretary of State was directed to promote the enhancement of human rights as a fundamental foreign policy objective. The Department was also asked to prepare reports on the status of human rights in all countries receiving U.S. aid.

The Carter Administration

With the inauguration of President Carter, the full power of presidential leadership was thrown into the struggle for human rights worldwide, and an era of renewed and heightened emphasis on human rights in American foreign policy began. This emphasis was clear in the President's inaugural address:

Our commitment to human rights must be absolute. . . . Because we are free we can never be indifferent to the fate of freedom elsewhere. Our moral sense dictates a clear-cut preference for those societies who share with us an abiding respect for individual human rights.

The rights defined by the Administration are based on international consensus. They fall into three categories:

☐ First, the right to be free from governmental violation of the integrity of the person. Such violations include torture; cruel, inhuman, or degrading treatment or punishment; arbitrary arrest or imprisonment; denial of fair public trial; and invasion of the home.

☐ Second, the right to fulfillment of such vital needs as food, shelter, health care, and education. The stage of a nation's economic development will obviously affect the fulfillment of this right. It can be violated, however, by a government's action or inaction—for example, by official corruption that diverts resources from a poor majority to a rich elite.

☐ Third, the right to enjoy civil and political liberties such as freedom of thought, religion, assembly, speech, and the press; freedom of movement both within and outside one's country; freedom to take part in government.

U.S. policy is to promote greater observance by all governments of these rights. They are all proclaimed in the Universal Declaration of Human Rights adopted by the United Nations a generation ago. And as President Carter told the United Nations: ". . . All the signatories of the United Nations Charter have pledged themselves to observe and to respect basic human rights. Thus, no member of the United Nations can claim that mistreatment of its citizens is solely its own business. Equally, no member can avoid its responsibilities to review and to speak when torture or unwarranted deprivation occurs anywhere in the world . . ."

Since 1945 international practice has confirmed that a nation's obligations to respect human rights are a matter of concern in international law. The United Nations, for example, has repeatedly dealt with human rights developments in individual states, such as the race conflict in South Africa.

The American obligation under the U.N. Charter, moreover, is written into U.S. legislation. Since 1976 the Foreign Assistance Act has read: "A principal goal of the foreign policy of the United States is to promote the increased observance of internationally recognized human rights by all countries." Other statutes direct the executive branch to apply human rights criteria to a broad spectrum of programs of foreign assistance and arms transfers. Present policy is thus in harmony with America's tradition, its international obligations, and its domestic laws.

THE REQUIREMENTS OF REALISM

A successful human rights policy must bear in mind the limits to American power and wisdom, and must be realistically shaped to each case that comes to hand. In each case it must answer the following questions:

First, what is the nature of the problem? What kind of violations are there? What is their extent? Is there a pattern? If so, is the trend toward concern for human rights or away from it? What is the degree of governmental control and responsibility? Is the government willing to allow independent, outside investigation?

Second, what are the chances for effective action? Will a proposed action promote the overall cause of human rights? Will it really improve the specific conditions? Is the other country receptive to U.S. interest and efforts? Will others cooperate, including official and private international organizations in the human rights field? Finally, does the U.S. sense of values and decency demand that we speak out or take action anyway, even though in the short run there is only a remote chance of influencing developments?

Third, does a proposed course avoid self-righteousness and stridency, bearing in mind that America's own record is not unblemished? Is it sensitive to genuine security interests, recognizing that outbreaks of armed conflict or terrorism could themselves threaten human rights? Does it take into account all the rights at stake?

Realism compels recognizing that U.S. actions may provoke retaliation against short-term U.S. interests, or sometimes even against the victims of repression themselves. Finding positive and creative ways to encourage governments to respect human rights is far better than penalizing them for poor performance. But when improvements do not ensue, governments must understand that there are costs to continued repression.

It is also realistic to recognize that unless U.S. domestic actions reflect a firm commitment to human rights, the message being sent to others will ring hollow. The Administration is taking steps to improve the U.S. human rights record. It has removed all restrictions on U.S. citizen travel abroad, and greatly eased visa requirements for foreigners coming to this country . . .

APPROACHES TO OTHER COUNTRIES

Our object is to improve human rights conditions abroad, not to embarrass others or publicize U.S. successes. When it becomes necessary to address human rights conditions in another country, therefore, the first step is to raise the matter in private with the government involved. This enables the other government to respond in private.

Sometimes the response is truculent and defensive. The United States is charged with "intervening" in the internal affairs of another sovereign state. But often there is a real effort to join issue on the merits. Governments are beginning to acknowledge the validity of the U.S. interest—an interest rooted in agreements that make the way a government treats its own citizens a matter of international concern.

Just as frequently there is disagreement over the seriousness and causes of the problem. But usually such differences can be bypassed by focusing on possible specific improvements, such as:

☐ Whether persons held without trial, perhaps incommunicado and for long periods, can soon be released or at least charged and given a fair public trial;
☐ Whether return to civilian rule can proceed on schedule; or
☐ Whether those responsible for mistreating prisoners will be prosecuted.

Sometimes explicit understanding can be reached on these issues. More often there is an implicit recognition of the need for improvement and for further consultations as the situation evolves. Raising the issue is significant in itself. Instead of being conveniently ignored, human rights abuses are brought to the center of the diplomatic interchange. There, they must be addressed.

The words of human rights diplomacy can be joined with symbolic acts. For example, trips to other countries by senior U.S. officials, and offical invitations to foreign leaders to visit the United States, can be used to recognize a country's outstanding human rights record or to provide a chance to talk over human rights problems with the leader of a country where improvements are needed.

Meetings with opposition leaders from countries with human rights problems can likewise be used to send signals to the governments of these countries. U.S. officials have met with several such leaders in Washington, including some living in exile. And abroad, U.S. Ambassadors regularly meet with opposition leaders. These meetings enable us to hear both sides of the story, to learn how a human rights problem is seen by those directly affected, and to show that the United States is concerned about all the people of the other country, not just those in power.

Beyond private discourse and symbolic steps, the diplomacy of human rights must sometimes include criticism of regimes that commit serious violations. Public comment by the U.S. Government is an official act that calls international attention to the practices of another government. We do not prefer this approach, but we will use it when necessary.

Public comment has necessarily been the first line of approach to countries like Cambodia [Kampuchea] and Uganda. The United States has little or no diplomatic contact with these governments, which have committed gross violations of human rights as a matter of deliberate state policy. We hope that other nations also will continue to drive home the extent of international concern and bring about improvements.

The United States has also spoken openly and forthrightly at the Belgrade meeting which reviewed implementation of the Helsinki Final Act. The act contemplates full and frank review of how the signatories have lived up to their human rights commitments. The Soviet Union and the East European countries, in varying degrees, have been delinquent. U.S. representatives at Belgrade did not hesitate to say so publicly, request explanations, and seek compliance. U.S. comments and those of West European governments have helped sustain the Helsinki accord as a living force for encouraging governments to respect the rights of their people. Silence would have allowed that force to fade away.

The tools of public diplomacy available to the U.S. International Communication Agency are also useful in conveying human rights concerns to nongovernmental audiences abroad. For example, the Voice of America has increased its attention to these issues.

The U.S. human rights initiative has given a boost to the longstanding efforts of private organizations such as the Red Cross, Amnesty International, and the International League for Human Rights. The U.S. Government works closely with these organizations and recognizes that over time, their efforts may well outdistance those of any government.

When the United States gives economic or military assistance to another government, it is in a position to take tangible steps to recognize good human rights performance or show concern over violations. In taking such steps, the Administration is guided by legislative provisions enacted by a Congress strongly committed to human rights.

Taking account of the needs of the poorest, a fundamental decision has been made gradually to channel a growing share of U.S. assistance to governments that respect the rights of their people. On the other hand, when recipients of U.S. aid repeatedly curtail human rights, and diplomatic efforts have failed, then restrictions are considered, both on overall aid levels and on individual loans or grants. Measures that have been taken include deferring bilateral economic or military assistance, opposing loans by the World Bank or other international financial institutions, and insuring that U.S. food aid reaches the people who need it.

Possible measures are not limited to aid. The Export-Import Bank, for example, takes human rights considerations into account in making loans. Commercial arms sales subject to government licensing receive similar scrutiny, and other trade restrictions may sometimes be considered.

Because of differences in culture and in economic and political maturity, imposing sanctions often presents painful choices. And human rights, while a fundamental factor in U.S. foreign policy, cannot always be the decisive factor. But there are times when, although the decision is difficult, the United States must continue to back up its words with actions.

COOPERATIVE EFFORTS

In pursuing the diplomacy of human rights, the United States works together with many governments in the United Nations, the Organization of American States, and other forums. We consult regularly with our West European allies and others on promoting broader international cooperation on human rights. We have found strong support for giving human rights a higher priority in international affairs . . .

In the Organization of American States, the United States has worked with many Latin American countries to strengthen the Inter-American Commission on Human rights. Several countries have informed the Commission they are willing to receive inspection visits, and several such visits have been made.

In the United Nations, the United States has joined with Venezuela and others in supporting the Costa Rican proposal to create a U.N. High Commissioner of Human Rights. We are also working with interested nations to try to add more force to the Declaration Against Torture adopted by the General Assembly in 1975.

SIGNS OF PROGRESS

U.S. human rights policy rarely can be viewed as a single cause for change in other countries. Many changes would take place regardless of what the United States did; many forces are at work of which U.S. policy is only one. But there have been signs of progress, and U.S. policy has made a contribution.

☐ First, promotion of human rights is no longer a relative stranger to the front pages of the world's newspapers. The message of U.S. concern has reached governments, their citizens, and the victims of repression themselves. There has been a heightening of international sensitivity to human rights, a freshening of the atmosphere.

☐ Second, governments are increasingly beginning to weigh the costs of repression—the damage it can do to their relations with the United States and other countries, and to their image in the world community.

☐ Third, from many regions, there have been concrete indications of forward movement. Thousands of political prisoners have been freed in over a dozen countries. Torture of prisoners has been reduced and trials are more often open to the public. In a number of cases, the process of broadening press and political freedom has started. The United States does not claim credit for these improvements; when a country makes progress in human rights, this is the result of decisions made by its people and its government. But U.S. policy has helped create a climate in which such changes may be more likely.

Finally, beyond its essential humanitarian purpose, our renewed attention to human rights advances U.S. interests in other ways. By demonstrating that our foreign policy truly reflects our national values, it has restored some lost luster to the American image . . .

The cause of human liberty, as Archibald MacLeish wrote in our bicentennial year, is the one great revolutionary cause. Our founding ideals, grounded in respect for human liberty, remain the most powerful in the world. And our fidelity to these ideals is the core of our strength as a nation.

The Task Ahead

As Lao Tzu observed, a journey of a thousand miles must begin with a single step. And every political prisoner released or fairly tried, every torturer forced to seek other employment, every child given a textbook, every farmer given better seed marks another step on a long journey—a journey our nation began two centuries ago in Philadelphia, when a small band of dissidents made the extraordinary claim that all men are created equal and endowed by their Creator with certain unalienable rights.

The distance covered is dwarfed by that which remains to be traveled. Instead of progress there is sometimes retrogression, and tragic human rights violations persist across the globe. Too many people are still subject to torture and suffering in squalid prisons, uncharged and untried. Too many are hungry and poorly sheltered, without adequate medical care or schools for their children. Too many are living under martial law or are otherwise barred from political participation. Too many are denied the right to emigrate or even to travel freely within their own countries.

These problems are the challenges of the future. They will not be easily solved. But the U.S. experience with human rights diplomacy has shown that while progress is difficult, it is not impossible.

BILL OF RIGHTS DAY, HUMAN RIGHTS DAY AND WEEK, 1980[4]

A Proclamation

On December 15, 1791, the Bill of Rights became part of the Constitution of the United States. On December 10, 1948, the United Nations General Assembly adopted the Universal Declaration of Human Rights. Marking these anniversaries together gives us an opportunity to renew our dedication both to our own liberties and to the promotion of human rights everywhere.

[4] Proclamation signed by Jimmy Carter, from Department of State Bulletin. United States. Department of State. Washington, DC 20520. F. '81. p 54.

The Bill of Rights carries with it an implied responsibility for the governed as well as for the governing. No American citizen can rest satisfied until the Bill of Rights is a living reality for every person in the United States, irrespective of race, religion, sex, national or ethnic origin. We cannot simply rely on the decency of government or the alertness of an active free press. Each individual must shoulder his or her share of the responsibility for seeing that our freedoms will survive.

The Universal Declaration of Human Rights is the cornerstone of a developing international consensus on human rights. Through it, the members of the United Nations undertake to promote, respect and observe human rights and fundamental freedoms for all without discrimination. We must continuously monitor the progress of this effort and the records of governments around the world.

The promise of the Declaration is remote to all those who suffer summary executions and torture, acts of genocide, arbitrary arrest and imprisonment, banishment, internal exile, forced labor and confinement for political cause. It is remote to the countless refugees who flee their lands in response to the elimination of their human rights. It is remote to those subjected to armed invasions or to military coups that destroy democratic processes. The Declaration will ring hollow to that segment of a population discriminated against by laws of *apartheid* or by restrictions on religious freedom. It will ring hollow to those threatened by violations of freedom of assembly, association, expression and movement, and by the suppression of trade unions.

The Declaration must also ring hollow to the members of the U.S. Embassy staff who have been held captive for more than a year by the government of Iran.

The cause of human rights is embattled throughout the world. Recent events make it imperative that we, as Americans, stand firm in our insistence that the values embodied in the Bill of Rights, and contained in the Universal Declaration, be enjoyed by all.

I urge all Americans to support ratification of the Geno-

cide Convention, the Convention on the Elimination of all
Forms of Racial Discrimination, the Covenant on Economic,
Social and Cultural Rights, the Covenant on Civil and Political Rights and the American Convention on Human Rights. I
renew my request to the Senate to give its advice and consent
to these important treaties.

NOW THEREFORE, I, JIMMY CARTER, President of the
United States of America, do hereby proclaim December 10,
1980, as Human Rights Day and December 15, 1980, as Bill of
Rights Day, and call on all Americans to observe Human
Rights Week beginning December 10, 1980. It should be a
time set apart for the study of our own rights, so basic to the
working of our society, and for a renewal of our efforts on behalf of the human rights of all peoples everywhere.

IN WITNESS WHEREOF, I have hereunto set my hand this
fourteenth day of November, in the year of our Lord nineteen
hundred and eighty, and of the Independence of the United
States of America the two hundred and fifth.

RIGHTS: ASSERT OR LOSE[5]

The phrase civil liberties has a long history in English and
American political usage, but it was the American Civil Liberties Union that first adopted it in an organization's title and
so brought it into a wider public vocabulary. Civil liberties
has always described the freedoms of the people in a democracy to speak, publish and organize.

They are what many schools of political thought call natural rights, the inherent desires of people to express themselves
and associate with their fellows. If strictly defined, they
would, I think, come out thus: Civil liberties, asserted as a
principle, become legal rights when they are embodied in en-

[5] Reprint of article by the late Roger N. Baldwin, founder of the American Civil
Liberties Union. New York *Times*. p A17. Ag. 31, '81. © 1981 by The New York Times
Company. Reprinted by permission.

forceable law, as they are in the Bill of Rights. The Bill of Rights covers all the protections of citizens against Government power abuses of the liberties of the people. It includes all the elements of fairness in the area of criminal justice, embodied in the phrase due process.

All rights of the people are restraints of Government or guarantees to the people by Government. They are individual, personal or collective, as the right of association. They find their political sanction in the supremacy of a sovereign people over their governments in a democracy. They find their judicial sanction in the protection of minority and personal rights against the majority. They find their philosophical sanction in the natural right of every individual to the fullest opportunity to develop his capacities. This purpose led Justice Louis Brandeis once to observe that "the fundamental human right is the right to be left alone."

Obviously, the application of these general principles raises constant and highly controversial questions: Conflicts of rights, the precedence of one right over another, the proper powers of Government, the social limits of personal freedoms—to name a few.

Democracy is choice; freedom of choice demands dissent, diversity, difference, all the contradictory counsels through which a majority arrives at a decision through public debate by press, radio, television and meetings of parties and organizations. This is the assumption underlying the A.C.L.U. activities for political freedom.

Without courage to assert rights, they weaken. The test of progress in American liberties is to be found in the determination of organized citizens to get and hold the rights they are presumed to have. Every minority won such rights as it has only by struggle, by organization, by insistence that its claims be recognized. "When liberty dies in the hearts of people," wrote Judge Learned Hand, "no constitutions and no laws will save it."

The task is to help nourish that spirit of liberty in the American people, to aid those who demand that the promises of democracy be fulfilled, to proclaim that the rights of all depend on the rights of each, not to suffer without action the slightest invasion of liberties in the conviction that to tolerate one is dangerous to all.

RIGHTS AND THE REAGAN ADMINISTRATION[6]

The State Department let it be known recently that, following the rejection by the Senate Foreign Relations Committee of Mr. Ernest Lefever as the Assistant Secretary of State for Human Rights and Humanitarian Affairs, it may simply leave that post unfilled. This apparent decision sheds light on the Administration's nomination of Lefever in the first place and on its attitude toward human rights in general. In the course of the debate over the nomination, the Administration argued that "quiet diplomacy" should be substituted for the Carter Administration's often public displays of disapproval of human-rights abuses in other countries, and that Mr. Lefever was the right man to effect the change. But in leaving the post vacant the Administration has now unmistakably signalled that all diplomacy, whether of the quiet or the outspoken kind, in favor of human rights is, at the very least, being sharply downgraded. In a way, though, having the post vacant will hardly be different from having Mr. Lefever in it, for on many occasions before he was nominated he had assailed the wisdom of including in American foreign policy human-rights considerations in any form. It is thus no reflection on his ability to say that having nobody serve instead of him in the post is quite fitting. His subsequent appointment as a consultant to the State Department on terrorism brings the whole story to a neat conclusion, since Secretary of State Alexander Haig has said that in the Administration concern about terrorism will "take the place of" concern about human rights. In his new post, Mr. Lefever will at least be

    [6] Reprint of magazine article entitled "Notes and Comment." *New Yorker*. 57:27. Jl. 20, '81. Reprinted by permission; © 1981 The New Yorker Magazine, Inc.

able to address himself to something that both he and the Administration are unquestionably worried about.

The Administration's human-rights policy has lately been further clarified by some remarks by Edwin Meese, the counsellor to the President, in an interview with Meg Greenfield, of the Washington *Post*, in which he defends an earlier allegation of his that the American Civil Liberties Union is a "criminals' lobby." In the interview, he describes himself as a strong believer in the Bill of Rights but goes on to reveal an apparent serious misconception of what political rights are and what role they play in our democracy. Describing the A.C.L.U. and a few other organizations as being "opposed to law enforcement," he proposes the establishment of "a comparable citizen group that represents the law-abiding citizens," which would oppose the A.C.L.U. "on the basis of the rights of the law-abiding citizen to be free from criminal activity." In a country that includes a Bill of Rights in its Constitution, however, rights *are* laws, and their enforcement is just as much law enforcement—and just as much in the interest of the law-abiding citizen—as the statutes against murder, burglary, assault, and other crimes. The difference is that the Bill of Rights was designed to protect citizens, on the whole, against the power of the government, whereas the criminal laws largely protect them against one another. (It is much easier for the government to silence a newspaper or prevent an individual from speaking than for another individual to do so.) The protection of the citizens from the power of government is an essential part of the idea of democracy, which places the government under the over-all scrutiny and supervision of the people. On the other hand, the citizens' need to be "free from criminal activity" (that is, from non-governmental criminal activity) is not, in the legal sense, a "right" at all (and thus is nowhere mentioned in the Bill of Rights) but, rather, an essential social good, like fire prevention, or adequate medical care, or the prevention of famine. Mr. Meese's devotion to what he thinks human rights to be is no doubt strong, but his definition of them is at odds with what the Constitution defines as rights. However, his views are of a piece with the views that other members of the Administration hold on human rights in foreign policy. An Administration that regards a citizens' lobby for human rights in the United States as a "criminals' lobby" could not be expected to fight for the establishment of a similar "criminals' lobby" in Argentina or El Salvador. Only confusion could result were it to champion abroad that which it does not favor at home.

II. INTERNATIONAL SURVEY

EDITOR'S INTRODUCTION

In this second section, our survey of human rights around the world starts with Marci McDonald's terrifying, wide-ranging report in *Maclean's* on human rights violations in Chile, Zaire, Kampuchea, Vietnam, Iraq, and the Soviet Union, to name but a few countries. The writer postulates that "in wielding human rights as a club, [the West may] have unsheathed a double-edged sword." As West and East confront each other on this issue, Nobel Peace Prizewinner Sean MacBride regrets: "It would be all right if it were furthering human rights, but all this is being used for propaganda purposes."

The next two articles report on a global basis year-to-year changes in the world population's freedom. While the State Department in its annual survey of human rights, as required by Congress, finds conditions improved overall throughout 1980, the yearly survey of Freedom House details numerically that the percentage of people living in freedom dropped from 1980 to 1981.

Writing in the British publication *World Today*, Edy Kaufman states that in Latin America "the scale of repression has been much greater during the last ten years than in any earlier period of the twentieth century . . . Not only do these escalating numbers [of human rights violations] mark the emergence of a new dark era, but qualitatively, too, the methods of repression and the choice of victims have become far more diversified." However, the writer is hopeful that "by 1980 the worst of the nightmare was over."

In the next selection the focus is on anti-Semitism in Argentina in light of the controversy ignited by publication of Jacobo Timerman's book *Prisoner Without a Name, Cell Without a Number* recounting his Argentine prison experiences. A second article also reports on human rights violations in Argentina, in particular, the plight of the thousands of desaparecidos (vanished ones), predominantly non-Jewish, and the arrest of human rights activist, Emilio Mignone, who had testified on their behalf before the UN Commission on Human Rights.

The final article by Michael Novak, U.S. representative to the UN Human Rights Commission, describes "the darkness of Orwellian doublespeak" at the Commission's annual meeting in Geneva. "Arguments over human rights, once they have been politicized as here they are, are not like any other . . . Human rights are of the spirit." He gloomily concludes that "Human rights as we understand them are not yet strangled to death, but cold fingers are on their windpipe."

THE GLOBAL STRUGGLE FOR HUMAN RIGHTS[1]

Spring had fallen softly on Santiago when they came for her—11 men with guns thundering down upon the tiny student café, dragging Ines Angelica Diaz Tapia screaming into an unmarked car. Four days later, her sister caught sight of her before a military tribunal, ravaged beyond her 25 years, her dark beauty unrecognizable. She was unable to stand upright. In those four days earlier this year in a "café house" of the central Nacional de Informaciones, one of Chile's secret services, she had been stripped and chained to the metal torture grid called the *parillo*. Slowly, with the exquisite attention to detail of the truly professional, they had beaten her all over her body, twisting their lighted cigarettes into her breasts and thighs.

Each time she passed out with the pain, she awoke to a doctor's ministrations. He did not dress her wounds but revived her to assure that she was conscious for the worst that was yet to come: the searing jolts of an electric shock rod

[1] Reprint of magazine article by Marci McDonald, Canadian correspondent for *Maclean's* in Paris. *Maclean's*. 93: 25–30. N. 24, '80. Copyright 1980 by Maclean-Hunter. Reprinted by permission.

roaming her flesh, then rammed deep into her private parts. In court, when she tried to cry out to her sister, an attendant slammed her across the face and led her away. For that pitiable bleat, she was held five days more, before being released to a women's detention centre where she languishes still, during what is termed a secret trial.

In the catalogue of testaments that trickle daily out of every corner of the globe on man's awesome capacity for inhumanity, the case of Ines Angelica Diaz Tapia is one of the less monstrous offerings. She, after all, lives to tell her tale—survives to awaken each night screaming with the souvenirs of her voyage into the murkiest sewers of the human spirit—her cry heard by that small band of the perpetually outraged who subscribe to Amnesty International's monthly newsletter.

But around the world, other wails will never be heard: the 15,000 Argentines declared officially "disappeared" since they were hauled out of their beds or assembly lines or even their detention camp cells and ominously promised a "transfer"; the hundreds of political opponents of Zaire's General Mobutu Sese Seko who, if not massacred or hung for their audacity in returning home to a promised amnesty, have perished of hunger, malnutrition and untreated disease in the torrid squalor of equatorial prison camps which not infrequently forgo the luxury of one meal a day.

Network news cameras numb the horrors from Asia: the slow sure genocide of two million Kampucheans by systematic starvation and murder. In the Middle East, the nightly firework spectaculars of a suicidal war overshadow the savagery tamed by statistics: 100 Iraqis put to death in a six-week period earlier this year, including the 50-year-old Ayatollah Muhammad Baqr al Sadr, most of them for the crime of simply being Shi'ite Moslems; more than 1,100 Iranians dispatched to execution squads without real defence or appeal by the contemptuous revolutionary tribunals that have succeeded in replacing the shah's bloody reign of terror with their own.

If those voices have been suffocated—often for merely

posing the most fundamental of questions, or holding a belief that did not please—it is nonetheless disconcerting to note that had they lived to rage against their fate, their cry would never have penetrated the broadloomed conference theatre of Madrid's Palacio de Congresos, where the diplomatic muscle of 35 nations gathered last week in an international tug-of-war over human rights.

As that tussle swells into a major confrontation of West against East, the tragedy may be that human rights themselves become a political club lost in the confusion of the fray. As former Irish foreign affairs minister Sean MacBride, an old soldier in the human rights wars and a Nobel Peace Prize winner, puts it: "It would be all right if it were furthering human rights, but all this is being used for propaganda purposes." Says Dr. Bernard Kouchner, France's 40-year-old "human rights doctor" who organized the hospital boat Ile de Lumière, which saved thousands of Vietnamese refugees from fetid death rafts: "Human rights has become a gadget."

Ever since the Soviet Union pushed for a European conference on security in Helsinki five years ago to win official sanction for their post-war boundaries, they have found themselves saddled with the astonishing trade-off of a commitment to protect their citizens' civil liberties which they never expected anyone to take so seriously. As pressure from dissidents within and Jimmy Carter's evangelistic foreign policy without mounted, the Kremlin's enraged backlash of repression surprised only those who failed to see that a system founded on the revolutionary ruminations of Karl Marx would be the first to realize that men with ideas are more dangerous than those with pistols.

As the Madrid conference opened, a rush of two dozen discreet post-Olympic trials clamped stiff prison sentences on the final larynges left to dissent—the names of journalists, Lithuanian and Ukrainian leaders and orthodox priests were added to that tragic 10,000-strong rollcall of the Soviet Union's best and brightest who have been silenced by enforced exile, psychiatric wards or the frozen hell of one of the Gulag Archipelago's 1,000-plus labor camps. Last Wednesday, when Olympian white-bearded novelist Lev Kopelev, who had survived Stalin's prisons, boarded a flight to Frankfurt on a one-year visa that is expected to turn into lifelong banishment, the ragtag band who saw him off at Moscow airport crumpled into tears and despair. His departure, coupled with the sudden death of exiled writer Andrei Amalrik in a freak car accident en route to the Madrid conference, were like twin fists which pummelled the last breath from the dissident dream of freedom.

The toll of recent repression has led more than one critic to question whether the whole Helsinki process hasn't hurt human rights more than it helped. Others warn that the West may well discover that, in wielding human rights as a club, they have unsheathed a double-edged sword. "If the U.S. can focus attention on violations of human rights, then all to the good," says MacBride. "But it must stop supporting these surrogates in Latin America who kill and torture people by the thousands. It's financing them, training the torturers in police colleges. It must put its own house in order."

Indeed, in their kit bag of Madrid diversions, the Soviets have a handy stock of American sins: discrimination against blacks, Mexicans and Puerto Ricans and, most damning of all, the news that the United States is the only major power that—thanks to a Senate standoff—has failed to ratify the International Genocide Convention, as well as 30 other assorted human rights pacts, all fastidiously signed by the Soviets.

In Europe, the backup squad, the French Communist party, has burrowed gleefully through the files of Amnesty International—the London-based human rights organization that tries to stay out of politics—to come up with France's treatment of Breton nuclear power demonstrators and West Germany's penchant for psychologically debilitating isolation cells. Britain already stands twice condemned of torturing suspected terrorists in Northern Ireland interrogation centres.

But in the mutual mudslinging that threatens to erupt between East and West in Madrid, the risk is that the terrible itemizations of torture, murder and legalized hate that fester in Africa, Asia and Latin America will be ignored or undermined. "If human rights are seen as a point in the cold war, it will tend to divide the Third World," says Thomas Hammerberg, Amnesty's new secretary-general. "We would hate a situation where most of the Third World countries came out against human rights because of superpower pressure—because they were financially dependent on one of the giants." As the Third World War seems already under way—a battle for men's minds fought with food aid and ideas in a series of quick brush-fire clashes—the body count continues to mount.

How to number the dead in South Korea, list the cadavers dumped into mass Vietnamese graves since Ho Chi Minh's legions marched into Saigon with flowers sprouting from their rifles? In Ethiopia today, there are estimated to be 100 times more political prisoners than during the most repressive of Emperor Haile Selassie's frenzies. In Chad, Uganda and the Central African Empire, one regime gives way to another but the dead still litter the deserts and the jungles.

The technology that hurtled man to the moon and spawned babies in test tubes has also devised subtler, more sophisticated cruelties. When Peter Benenson, a London lawyer with a social conscience, launched Amnesty on May 28, 1961, the world was a simpler place of "forgotten prisoners of conscience" languishing uncharged, untried and, in many cases, unidentified in the world's jails. Now, as the organization enters its 20th year, it is faced with combatting an insidious and frequently undocumentable new face of horror—the enigmatic official "disappearances" and confinements to asylums, the sleek updated torture chambers that specialize in electric and psychological tinkering leaving no telltale scars, only broken spirits and psyches. "Now governments blame executions on terrorism," says Hammerberg. "Political opponents are marked by death squads who are very close to the authorities. Or they plant drugs on them or invent false rape charges. It makes our work more difficult. In a case of psychiatric abuse, how do you find out the real background?"

Guatemala can boast that it has no political prisoners, but in the last decade at least 20,000 political opponents—many of them stubborn trade union leaders—have been eliminated by paramilitary death squads. Last September, Amnesty succeeded in documenting the deaths of three Iraqis who died promptly after their release from jail with a parting glass of orange juice or yogurt—the victims of thallium, a rat poison that produces an excruciating agony.

Third World leaders such as India's Indira Gandhi, who has just fallen back on her old emergency measures nightstick, argue that the West's vaunted liberties are luxuries they cannot afford in unstable societies floundering under poverty and illiteracy. "Nonsense," retorts MacBride, who heard the argument most recently during his three-year study of the international media for UNESCO. "There is nothing that creates instability quicker than the brutalization of a population. Iran is a perfect example." Iran, in fact, illustrates the human rights conundrum. But as Amnesty spokesman Richard Reoch points out: "What's happening in Iran now doesn't mean the shah's regime was more humane. It only means the problem is still there." Iran has become the textbook example of the difficulty of translating morality into realpolitik—an effort the embryonic Reagan administration already seems all too willing to forgo.

Last week, as the debate droned on in Madrid, David Rockefeller, chairman of Chase Manhattan Bank and friend of the former shah, flew off on what appeared to be unofficial gladhanding to reassure the Latin American juntas with the worst torture records—Chile, Argentina, Paraguay and Brazil—that Reagan "will deal with the world as it is. He is not going to try to change the world in his own image."

Nevertheless, when critics ponder whether human rights ought to be soft-pedalled for the sake of preserving the frail spider's web of détente to which they cling, the loudest rallying cry to slog on has come from those who are suffering most for the price of the issue having become a political football: the dissidents themselves. From his bleak exile in Gorki, Andrei Sakharov survives police beatings and harassment to launch the call: "Our only protection is the spotlight of public attention." From the merciless bowels of a Soviet forced-labor camp, Yuri Orlov risks death to smuggle out word of his hunger strike begun last week and to urge the West to hold the Soviet Union accountable for its violations of the promises made in Helsinki.

The danger is that as the economic crisis turns the West toward conservatism and navel-gazing, human rights will pass the way of all fads—a kind of moral crunchy granola which has lost its novelty and political expediency. In the end, as MacBride points out, it must come down to the individual "who is willing to stand up and be counted." Amnesty acts on just that principle: adopt three prisoners of conscience and lobby for them before taking on the world. "If I have managed to save one man from being hanged," says Hammerberg, who reads the bad news from the front lines of the human rights wars daily, "then it's worth it all." It is the viewpoint shared by Bernard Kouchner, the "human rights doctor" who founded Médecins Sans Frontières and its breakaway group, Médecins du Monde, with teams of French doctors treating the wounded in the political minefields of El Salvador and Afghanistan. "The first law of human rights," he says, "is to prevent a man from dying." Kouchner rages against institutionalized charity, "where everybody shrugs off the responsibility and says the Red Cross will cope." Two years ago, when nobody was going to the Southeast Asian seas to throw a lifeline to the thousands adrift in their own despair and vomit, he organized the Ile de Lumière against official opposition from all sides—now hailed as the West's humanitarian triumph. "You can't say, 'I can do nothing,' " he explodes over a Paris bistro table. "You must say, 'I can do anything.' There's so much misery in the world, one must throw oneself into it to defy our own deaths. In the Third World, it's ourselves we seek. You take one sick man in charge, you take up the cause of one prisoner, you dig one village well. One for one. A man for a man." Peter Benenson put it another way. He launched his band of faithful with a Chinese proverb: "Better to light a candle than curse the darkness."

U.S. REPORT SAYS STATUS OF RIGHTS IMPROVED DURING '80[2]

The State Department's annual survey of human rights reported today that torture, disappearances, and inhuman treatment of prisoners had continued to decline during the last year of the Carter Administration.

The report, prepared by the former Administration, said the improved situation was particularly manifest in countries where human-rights violations came under "intense international scrutiny and criticism."

Under President Carter, United States officials frequently criticized foreign governments for human-rights violations, and restrictions were placed by Congress on United States military and economic aid to persistent violators.

President Reagan and Secretary of State Alexander M. Haig Jr. have said that the new Administration would emphasize "international terrorism" as the most serious human-rights violation.

The Soviet Union came under more serious criticism this year than in last year's report, largely because of Moscow's intervention in Afghanistan and domestic repression of dissidents.

"Soviet practices in Afghanistan which violated human rights have included the reported use of lethal chemical weapons, 'trick' explosives, and indiscriminate bombing and terrorizing of the Afghan population," the report said.

"Soviet authorities," it continued, "have also stepped up repression at home, in a crackdown on human rights activists as severe as any since the beginning of the human rights movement over a decade ago."

Vietnam was also singled out for persistent human rights violations, including the existence of labor camps holding

[2] Reprint of article by Juan de Onis, staff reporter. New York *Times*. p 10. F. 10, '81. © 1981 by The New York Times Company. Reprinted by permission.

more than 50,000 political prisoners, and the "at times
coerced departure of nearly 1 million Vietnamese" over the
last five years.

The report said human rights were also adversely affected
in Vietnam by "increased conscription and the worsening of
social and economic conditions" as a consequence of Vietnam's invasion of Cambodia.

The publication of this year's report, which detailed conditions in 153 nations, by the Senate Foreign Relations Committee and the House Committee on Foreign Affairs was de-
layed for a week at the request of Mr. Haig to avoid public
criticism of South Korea during the visit here last week of
President Chun Doo Hwan.

On South Korea, the report said that "after some improvement in the earlier part of the year, the observance of civil
and political rights in 1980 was marked by deterioration."

Under martial law declared on May 17, the report said
that a sweeping "purification" of society launched by the
Government had "sharply restricted the rights of politicians,
journalists, scholars and others."

The report said that the trial of Kim Dae Jung, South
Korea's leading opposition figure, whose death sentence has
been commuted under international pressure by President
Chun, was conducted in a manner that "seriously abridged
the right to effective counsel."

In Latin America, where the Carter Administration's
spotlight on human-rights violations provoked the resentment
of military rulers, this year's report showed particular concern over the political violence in El Salvador and Guatemala, and repression by the military in Bolivia after it overthrew a civilian Government.

El Salvador's military-backed Government has been unable to subdue a guerrilla movement led by "armed leftists
who are responsible for a large number of kidnappings for
ransom and murder of Government officials, diplomats and
landowners" or to control the "abuses of death squads and
other rightist terrorist groups which include present or re-
tired members of the military," said the report.

"Alarmed by reforms which attack the very basis of their

domination, the armed extreme right has declared its intention to bring down the Government and reestablish the old order through violence perpetrated by its supporters, some of whom are members of the security forces," the report said.

Bolivia's military regime, which seized power last July, "ended the progress that had been made in restoring constitutional democracy and destroyed the favorable human rights climate" that developed after an earlier military regime left power in 1977, the report said.

In contrast, the report's summaries on Argentina and Chile, which had come under heavy fire in previous reports, recorded improved human-rights situations, with a reduction of disappearances of persons after arrest by security forces. In Argentina, the report said there had been 28 cases of disappearances reported in 1980, compared with over 6,000 in the period from 1976 to 1979.

However, as in many other countries under permanent military rule by decree, the report said that Argentina and Chile represented a general lack of progress during 1980 "toward respect for political and civil freedoms in the world," despite a decline in the most violent repression of human rights.

South Africa's system of separate racial development received extensive analysis in the report, as well as South Africa's administration of the territory of South-West Africa, known as Namibia.

"Security laws were frequently used during 1980 to detain and convict persons involved in school boycotts, labor strikes, and the activities of black political organizations," said the report, which found that South African press reporting on internal security matters and black protest was more restricted than previously.

Liberia, where a military uprising led by non-commissioned officers overthrew and killed President William Tolbert in April, 1980, was treated gently in the report.

While noting the execution after "hasty trials" of 13 former high officials, the report said the "new Government came in with the expressed intention of raising the standard of living of the people and ending corruption."

The section on "Israel and the Occupied Territories" did not vary in any significant way this year from earlier reports. It said that Arabs under Israel rule "tend to feel powerless and largely alienated" but it said the Arab minority within Israel has "equal rights under the law" and is free of human-rights violations.

In the occupied West Bank and Gaza Strip, which are under military rule, the report noted that the establishment of 120 non-military settlements "has adversely affected the livelihood of some Arab residents" particularly where land and water rights have been transferred to the Jewish settlers.

FREEDOM DROPPED 1980–1981[3]

The percentage of people now living in freedom compared to last year dropped by 1.1 points to 35.9 percent of the world's population. There are 1,613 million persons residing in 51 free nations and 29 related territories. The percentage of partly free and not free increased. There are 970.9 million (21.6 percent) living in 76 partly free places, and 1,911.9 million (42.5 percent) residing in 62 countries and territories regarded as not free.

The human population has increased to 4,495.8 million, so that the number living in free countries rose while the percentage diminished.

In 17 countries with 1,455 million people, reductions in political rights and/or civil liberties were noted by our Comparative Survey of Freedom. In 7 of these, with populations of 68.7 million, deteriorations in human freedom moved the country to a lower category. Turkey and Upper Volta went from free to partly free; Surinam from free to not free; and Bolivia, Liberia, Seychelles, and Syria from partly free to not free.

The loss of freedom in 10 other nations with 1,380 million population was not sufficient to move the country to a lower

[3] Reprint of article entitled "Freedom in the World—1981." *Freedom At Issue.* 59:2. Ja.-F., '81. Copyright 1981 by Freedom House, Inc. Reprinted by permission.

category. Losses, however, were noted in partly free China (Taiwan), El Salvador, Grenada, Guatemala, Korea (South), and Western Samoa; and in not free China (Mainland), Haiti, the Soviet Union, and Zambia.

For 45.9 million persons in 4 countries there were major improvements in status. Ghana and Peru went from partly free to free, and Uganda and Uruguay from not free to partly free.

Improvements within categories were recorded for 8 countries with 123.3 million: Honduras, Nepal, Panama, Poland, Thailand, Vanuatu, and Zimbabwe among the partly free, and Iraq among the not free.

At the outset of 1981, the following levels of political rights and civil liberties are shown in our Comparative Survey:

Not free: 1,911.9 million (42.5 percent of the world's population), of whom 1,910.1 million live in 58 countries (35.8 percent of the nations), and 1.8 million reside in 4 (11.2 percent) of the related territories.

Partly free: 970.9 million (21.6 percent), of whom 962 million live in 53 nations (32.7 percent), and 8.9 million reside in 23 (41.1 percent) of the territories.

Free: 1,613 million (35.9 percent), of whom 1,607.6 million inhabit 51 countries (31.4 percent), and 5.4 million live in 29 (51.8 percent) of the related territories.

HUMAN RIGHTS IN LATIN AMERICA—A WATERSHED?[4]

Violations of human rights in Latin America have become a salient world issue not only because of a growing international awareness of the general problem, but also because the

[4]Reprint of article by Edy Kaufman, a member of the International Executive Committee of Amnesty International with responsibility for the Americas and Visiting Associate Professor at the University of California at Los Angeles. *World Today.* 37:63–8. F. '81. This article is reprinted by kind permission of *The World Today* (Vol. 37, No. 2, February 1981), monthly journal of the Royal Institute of International Affairs, London.

scale of repression has been much greater during the last ten years than in any earlier period of the twentieth century. The most dramatic quantitative increase can be seen in the figures for a country which had no level of government-instigated violence in the past but has one of the worst records at present: in Uruguay—formerly called 'the Switzerland of Latin America'—political imprisonment reached its peak four years ago, when 5,000 prisoners, comprising one out of every 500 citizens in this small country, were behind bars; probably as many as one out of 50 citizens has been interrogated by the military authorities.

However, figures given in reports of Amnesty International for Latin America show that, in recent years, the numbers of political prisoners began to decline. But this trend is accompanied by a sharp increase in the numbers of disappearances. It seems that most kidnapped persons have been killed; the fact that the bodies are not usually found, or if found are difficult to identify, makes it impossible to provide an accurate assessment; figures running into thousands in several countries may convey an impression of the magnitude of these problems. Argentina has an estimated 2,500 political prisoners, but the number of people who have disappeared (*desaparecidos*) is in the range of ten to twenty thousand. Documentary evidence exists for about 6,000 individual cases. In Chile, where the military takeover in 1973 produced an estimated 30,000 casualties, there are still 1,500 persons missing. In Guatemala, since 1966, about 25,000 individuals have disappeared or are known to be victims of extra-judicial executions. During the first six months of 1978, 770 unidentified bodies were discovered in unmarked graves in one cemetery alone. Furthermore, a Guatemalan National Police spokesman reported that, for the first ten months in 1979, figures of the killings by the Anti-Communist Secret Army were 3,252. The Somoza regime's legacy in Nicaragua is about 3,000 *desaparecidos*. In El Salvador, the survival of the new civic-military junta has been threatened by controversy over the demands of the whereabouts of around 400 cases of people who have disappeared: during its first year in power, it has been unable to stop, or has tolerated, a further 8,000 cases of political assassination.

Not only do these escalating numbers mark the emergence of a new dark era, but qualitatively, too, the methods of repression and the choice of victims have become far more diversified. In one South American country alone, we may find allegations about the use of the following instruments and methods of torture: electric prod, cigarette burnings, 'the submarine' (the head of the prisoner is submerged in water mixed with excrement until he is nearly asphyxiated); the 'dry submarine' (variation of the 'submarine' employing a plastic bag); *la capucha* (the person is kept hooded for months); *el caballete* (the prisoner is seated naked outdoors on an iron bar, his legs not touching the floor); *el plantón* (the victim is kept standing, legs apart for many hours or even days); the 'flag' (the prisoner is hanged by his hands, his legs not touching the floor); blows; the 'telephone' (a special blow given simultaneously on both ears); tearing out finger nails; sexual abuses; the 'grill' (parts of the body are exposed to burning charcoal); and the 'little pig' (the prisoner is put into a small wooden box with an iron bar in the middle, the mobile top allowing for gradual exertion of pressure on the back). Bodies of *desaparecidos* are often found with signs of torture—if they are found at all: for instance, there have been three reported cases of victims thrown alive from planes into the ocean with a heavy weight attached to their legs.

Repression has become so generalized that often only a minority of victims are known to have been active opponents of the established regimes. Family members, including babies, are kidnapped and disappear or are murdered. Such acts perform, perhaps, the 'rational' function of deterring potential dissenters, as well as the irrational one of revenge for the acts of the members of the family perceived to be responsible.

Another group which became a particular target of repression in Argentina has been the Jewish community. The large numbers of imprisoned and missing Jews (1,100 names are listed by the Anti-Defamation League) points to an exaggeration in the assessment of their involvement in 'subversive' activities, since this assessment can hardly be explained only in terms of a larger representation of Jews among opposition groups. A blatantly vindictive behaviour towards Jewish prisoners is documented in testimonies, such as the recently published report of Amnesty International about two secret detention camps in Argentina. People in specific professions have also been singled out for persecution, for example, lawyers and journalists in Argentina. Many of them were eliminated only because they were working competently within their professions. Merely defending an accused person in court has been considered proof of identification with the defendant. Psychiatrists have been tortured in order to force them to disclose information about patients. In Chile, a British woman doctor, Sheila Cassidy, was savagely tortured because she had provided medical assistance to opponents of the regime. Targets for repression can even be chosen according to a biological fact, such as age. In its report on Nicaragua released shortly before President Somoza's downfall, the Inter-American Commission on Human Rights found that the National Guard in Esteli, Diriamba and other places had repressed indiscriminately 'any male youth between 14 and 21 years of age'.

Some observers outside the region have raised the question of 'endemic' political violence in Latin America. But it should be pointed out that, even if elements of repression were prevalent in the past experience of these societies, the situation in recent years has acquired a distinctive character in both its scope and its intensity. In trying to analyze the causal factors of the present large-scale repression, one could find strong arguments based on the grave social problems inherent in the infrastructure of these countries. However, it is most important to acknowledge the effect of the polarization of political forces. Following the success of the Cuban revolution, expectations of revolutionary social change and redistribution of wealth—achieved through guerrilla tactics—were raised throughout Latin America. Radical forces challenged the existing political systems, military as well as civilian regimes, by exposing what they considered to be 'a state of latent violence' as measured by high rates of infant mortality, severe working conditions, low life expectancy and, in general terms, social injustices. The belief that revolutionary movements could provoke these regimes into open confrontation was then to provide them with the opportunity to unmask the 'true nature', the essentially repressive character of the established political power. Indeed, the reaction has been even stronger than expected, with military and paramilitary forces used by the regimes to crush not only the guerrilla fighters but also many other peaceful dissenters.

Polarization in Chile took a different form. The Allende government advocated a policy of rapid social change, which it implemented by stretching the existing legal framework to its furthest limits. While, on one hand, the rather undisciplined ruling coalition was pressurized by extreme-left elements inside and outside its ranks, on the other, this radical process brought about a consolidation of the opposition, with the centre sectors joining the forces favouring status quo and reaction. This confrontation led to a level of conflict which, in the eyes of a great part of the military élite, legitimized the coup d'état and subsequent repression.

Trend Reversal?

More generally, economic chaos, the deterioration of 'law and order', the active involvement of the United States in wide aspects of military and police training in Latin America, all were elements that accelerated the emergence of unprecedented repression. By 1976, 16 out of the 20 old Latin American republics were under direct or indirect military rule. However, by 1980 the picture had changed considerably, with a projection for 1981 of 11 countries back or on their way back to civilian rule. Torture by many of the most notorious users—such as Uruguay—has decreased considerably. Figures of political imprisonment have fallen drastically in Brazil, and disappearances have been significantly reduced in Chile and Argentina. Still, persecution of trade unionists, im-

prisonment of discontented Indians, and the widespread use
of torture seem to be on the increase in Colombia, and large
numbers of political prisoners and assassinations accompanied the 1980 coup in Bolivia. Furthermore, the focus of repression seems to have moved to Central America, with El
Salvador and Guatemala now undergoing a process comparable to the polarization that affected the Southern Cone some
years ago. However, overall observation for the end of the
1970s clearly pointed to a gradual recovery of basic freedoms.
When trying to assess the causes for the reversal of the trend,
a number of elements should be mentioned: no doubt, the
erosion of the power of the military, due both to their failure
to provide a model for rapid economic development and to
the frictions between generals, has led to a growing desire to
relinquish formal political responsibilities; furthermore, the
level of repression has resulted in such high costs in human
lives, suffering and exile that by now the 'job' has been quite
successfully consummated.

But other trends, too, have had a serious impact on human
rights in Latin America. The Church, in general, has become
identified with this struggle, being particularly conscious of
its central role when all other opposition forces were crushed.
Relatively more immune because of the proclaimed alle-
giance of the rulers to 'Christian' values, the clergy and its followers have been able not only to provide effective assistance
to the victims and their families but also to serve as an element of continuous criticism and denunciation. Local Human
Rights Committees launched by the Catholic Church have
rapidly become a uniting democratic force with both ecu-
menical and multi-party participation.

Rejecting previously established standards and practices,
the Carter Administration did initially play an important role
in furthering human rights in Latin America. Although the
policy has been under fire for being often too declaratory or
inconsistent, it was in Latin America that it found its highest
expression. For instance: hundreds of political prisoners were
released through the direct intervention of United States em-
bassies; states of siege or other restrictive legislation were

lifted in a number of countries; military aid for human rights violators either ceased or was reduced. In the Dominican Republic, the military leaders were pressured by the White House to accept the result of the elections, that is, the victory of the candidate associated with the social-democratic movement. In Bolivia, the United States repeatedly opposed the attempts at counter-coups by generals who wanted to stop the emerging civilian rule. Although much more could have been done, in comparison with the policies of previous United States administrations in relation to the problems in Latin America, it would be unfair not to acknowledge the new attitude of the Carter Administration and its serious impact on the continent.

However, after the performance of the first two years of the Administration, concern for human rights violations in Latin America decreased considerably. For example, arguments for renewing (as a stimulus to further liberalization) limited aid to regimes that have reduced—though not totally eradicated—grave violations of human rights, cannot be taken too seriously. The deterioration of East–West relations and the emergence of the Sandinistas as the victorious power in Nicaragua, were two of the factors that contributed to a change in the priorities of the White House. In addition, there was the presidential electoral campaign, in which a hawkish image was considered by some to be more conducive to success than a non-ideological open and flexible policy towards Latin America.

The prospects for a human rights policy under the Reagan Administration seem rather poor. The Republican platform included only two items concerning Latin America: the intention to defend the security interests of the United States in the Panama Canal, and expressions of concern about the 'Marxist' threat in Nicaragua. Statements by Mr. Reagan's Latin American advisers seem to point towards a policy of unrestricted arms sales to governments in the area regardless of the persistence of gross violations of human rights. This was already confirmed in the renewal of US military assistance to El Salvador's civic-military junta, at a time when persistent

allegations of the regime's involvement in massive and indiscriminate killings have been increasingly documented.

The positive role played by the international community
should be stressed. In a rather selective way, United Nations-
related governmental bodies have been exposing human
rights violations in some Latin American countries, particularly in the case of Chile. A more systematic, impartial and
continuous work has been carried out by non-governmental
voluntary organizations such as Amnesty International, the
International Commission of Jurists and others. Working for
the release of hundreds of individual cases of imprisoned dissenters, sending thousands of letters from all over the world in
response to allegations of torture, and exposing the assassinations and disappearances have not only produced an impact
on the governments concerned but also created a more informed international public opinion.

The activity of the Inter-American Commission on
Human Rights also deserves to be noted. From the time, a
decade ago, when the concerns of its members were being
defined only in critical reports on Cuba, to its active involvement today with nearly any country in the hemisphere pre-
senting human rights violations, the Commission has become
a major catalyst in the Organization of American States
(OAS)—resulting in the growing isolation of the most extreme
violators. With the cohesion of Latin America as a region encouraging a process whereby changes in one or a few countries are having repercussions in many others, a new policy
has rapidly been acquiring momentum. The cumulative effect of all these elements has strengthened the hand of Latin
American governments such as Ecuador, Venezuela and many
English-speaking small Caribbean states which have been
showing consistent concern in the defence of human rights
throughout the region. The steady growth of this block over
the last two years has brought a new coalition of forces in the
Organization of American States. In its General Assembly,
which took place in Bolivia's capital in October 1979, resolutions condemning disappearances (such as have occurred in
Argentina, El Salvador and Chile) as 'an affront to the con-

science of the hemisphere' and referring to torture (in Chile, Paraguay and Uruguay) received a majority of 19 votes, while only two voted against, five abstained and one was absent.

Cuba, though still formally an outsider to the Inter-American system, has also been indirectly affected by this general process. Castro has been faced with pressures arising not only from growing international concern but also from the greater awareness of his followers in Latin America, moulded by their personal experience, of the importance of respecting human rights. In response to these pressures and in an attempt to normalize relations with the United States, Fidel Castro announced the release of 3,000 political prisoners, a scheme that has now been wound up. Although many more hundreds remain in jail and a severe prison regime seems to be imposed on those who resist being placed under a system of 're-education', it is important to observe such changes of substance.

But one should beware of excessive optimism when assessing the present state of affairs. The result of the American elections has already had a noticeable impact on the most recent OAS General Assembly, which was convened in Washington in November 1980: Argentina, for instance, took the initiative to block the specific mention of human rights violators by threatening to withdraw from the organization, and a compromise was finally agreed upon. Similarly, the recent coup in Bolivia was hardly mentioned. Thus positive developments should be regarded in the context of a transition from the most repressive period of contemporary Latin American history to a state in which serious human rights violations persist in a large number of countries. So long as fundamental problems of social justice remain unsolved in most societies, tensions, instability and violence will not vanish.

Nor does the present de-escalation of repression necessarily mean that this will be also the trend in the future. The deterioration of détente, the decline of the human rights policy already under the Carter Administration and the entrenchment of the military in some of the Latin American regimes do not allow such sanguine predictions. Indeed, the process might even be reversed, if events in Central America were to provoke a direct confrontation with Washington. Nevertheless, the general feeling remains that by 1980 the worst of the nightmare was over. Historic memories of repression are likely to last for some time and help in shaping middle-of-the-road alternatives to political polarization. Whereas social, economic, and often civil and political rights will continue to be violated, this will not necessarily result in a large-scale rejection of fundamental human rights.

THE SIEGE OF THE ARGENTINE JEWS[5]

The controversy over the indictment of Argentine anti-Semitism by Jacobo Timerman, the former newspaper publisher and political prisoner, is better resolved by historical than by hysterical pleading. Too much of the current debate has been colored by the vogue for finding virtue in right-wing "authoritarian" regimes, as in Alexander Haig's recent embrace of the Argentine junta as God-fearing and anti-totalitarian. A mirror image of this disservice to reasoned discussion is the strident criticism of Argentina's treatment of Jews by certain leftist commentators who previously have displayed scant interest in combating anti-Semitism elsewhere, but an all too constant enthusiasm for pinpointing faults, real or imagined, of right-wing governments. As a final contribution to confusion, certain understandably intimidated Argentine Jewish leaders have been frantically denying that their government is at all anti-Semitic. The fact is, however, that there exists in Argentina today a salient pattern of anti-Semitic activities by both private elements and government agents, and it draws on prejudices found widely in Argentine society.

Timerman's own experience, during 30 months of military detention, is a striking illustration of the danger to which

[5] Reprint of magazine article by Robert Weisbrot, author of *The Jews of Argentina* and teacher of American history and foreign policy at Colby College. *New Republic.* 184:16–21. Je. 27, '81. Copyright 1981 by The New Republic, Inc. Reprinted by permission.

Jews in Argentina (variously estimated between 300,000 and a half a million) are vulnerable. A staunch Zionist and advocate of an "open society" despite the government's war against leftist guerrillas, he was anathema to key officers in the junta. Timerman was arrested without explanation in April 1977 and suffered repeated physical and psychological torture. In September 1979, some two years after the Argentine supreme court had first demanded his release, the junta had Timerman expelled from the country, still uninformed of any charges against him.

Some commentators who wish to avoid offending the Argentine junta have denied that Timerman's imprisonment is evidence of government anti-Semitism. They argue, as Argentine diplomats have argued almost since the junta's seizure of power over five years ago, that in a nation plagued by guerrilla terrorism, the military has been forced to take stern preventive security measures, affecting non-Jews as well as Jews. Some abuses of Jews and other prisoners have occurred, these commentators concede, but they are isolated incidents. They stress that, in general, only Argentines suspected of subversion have been targets of government forces.

Of course it is true that Jews are not the only ones to have suffered from terrorism in Argentina. The 15,000 *desaparecidos* (those who disappeared after government arrest, and are believed executed) and the thousands more killed by left- and right-wing guerrillas are predominantly non-Jews, including some Catholic priests. One Argentine said as early as 1972, "You could make a case that the country is anti-Argentine, if you look at all the victims of terrorism."

After every reasonable allowance is made for disruptive social conditions, however, one still finds that the mere fact of Jewish identity has stimulated government mistrust and often active harassment. Timerman's recent memoir of captivity, *Prisoner Without a Name, Cell Without a Number* (Knopf) [1981], records how his interrogators focused obsessively on presumed Zionist conspiracies, of which he, a prominent Jew, was thought to have intimate knowledge. Some comparatively restrained questioners postulated an imminent Israeli

commando raid to convert southern Argentina into a second
Jewish state. Others adhered to the more expansive if con-
ventional anti-Semitic fantasies of the *Protocols of the Elders
of Zion*, and asked for details on the alleged Jewish plot to
rule the world. During the tortures that alternated with these
inquisitions, Timerman's tormentors also routinely hurled
anti-Semitic epithets at him.

Lately some commentators have tried to discredit Timerman's charges of government anti-Semitism by resorting to
vicious *ad hominem* innuendoes. Essentially they seek to reduce the causes of Timerman's agony to his ties with David
Graiver, the late financier (also Jewish) alleged by the military to have channeled funds to terrorists. Although Graiver
had invested funds in Timerman's enterprises, it should be
noted that no one has ever adduced evidence that Timerman
had the slightest knowledge of any subversive activities. Indeed, the case against Graiver himself was based largely on
the replies of a captured guerrilla who was questioned under
torture by security agents. These charges still await proof.
Observers at the time noted that the Graiver affair enabled
the junta quickly to implicate many of its most prestigious
and troublesome opponents, including two former presidents
(Alejandro Lanusse and Isabel Perón) alleged to have obtained funds from Graiver's banks. Timerman was arrested
and his widely read journal, *La Opinión*, noted for its defenses
of Zionism and human rights, was confiscated by the military.

There is another indication that the Graiver affair was a rationale for Timerman's persecution rather than the cause of
it. The military continued to move against other Jews and
predominantly Jewish economic interests, even in the absence of this rationale. In May 1977 the military seized Aluar,
an important aluminum processing plant in which a major
shareholder was José Ber Gelbard, a Polish-born Jew and the
only person in the former civilian government to have been
exiled by the junta almost immediately after it took power.

Only the strongest defenders of the junta would suggest
that these purges against Timerman and other prominent
Jews were "coincidences" free of any anti-Semitic motiva-
tion. Yet since some commentators recently have passed this

test of human credulity, let us accept for the moment that the military acted solely on the grounds that Graiver was a suspected agent of terrorists, Timerman a suspected accomplice, and Gelbard conceivably a focal point of liberal resistance to military rule. Why, then, in this same period, was the American Jewish Committee office in Buenos Aires closed under duress, and why did its director, Jacobo Kovadloff, leave Argentina with his family after they were harassed and threatened by government security agents? Kovadloff, a humanistic Argentine leader, had long been respected as a nonpartisan worker concerned with interfaith toleration. Kovadloff, like other Argentine Jewish leaders, has refrained from public criticism of the government; yet his experience affirms Timerman's unshrinking accusations.

The recent flurry of attacks on Timerman's career and on his claim that the junta persecuted him as a Jew are not only unsound, they also divert attention from the dangers facing the Argentine Jewish community as a whole. Anti-Semitism in Argentina extends far beyond the victimization of a few prominent figures. Its manifestations are widespread and brutal, and it predates both Timerman's ordeal and the March 1976 coup that brought this particular junta to power.

Ever since Jews came from Europe to Argentina in large numbers during the late 19th century, they have found their adopted land a dangerously unstable host. They have enjoyed a large measure of cultural freedom and economic opportunity, and today comprise an educated and generally prosperous middle class in Argentine society. Yet recurrent surges of bigotry reveal a nation that has sometimes seemed a shelter less for Jews than for anti-Semites.

The terror eclipsing Jewish life over the decades has been prompted by various forms of violence and vandalism. Synagogue bombings, swastikas desecrating Jewish cemeteries, shootings, kidnappings, and virulent, well-financed propaganda campaigns have been among the recurring offenses. The perpetrators have also varied from hatemongers parading military insignia to Nazi war criminals to guerrilla bands on both political extremes.

Anti-Semitic attitudes, far from being confined to a few

extremist elements in the military and elsewhere, are widespread in Argentine society. Much of the disdain for Jews
stems from religious prejudice, though in a far less potent
form than in an earlier era of Latin American history (the
Spanish Inquisition was formally abolished in Argentina in
the early 1800s). Respected prelates and Catholic journals
like *Criterio* condemn anti-Semitism as un-Christian. But
subtler prejudices remain, such as sermons that perpetuate
themes such as the Jewish "Christ-killer" image.

The fact that most Jews are tradespeople and a substantial
number are professionals in a country chiefly composed of un-
skilled and semi-skilled laborers exacerbates tensions. The
economic success of many Jews has drawn hostility. Upper-
class Argentines often deride Jews as *nouveaux riches* who
lack the breeding of true gentlemen, and lower-class workers
refer to a car beyond their means as "the car of the Jews."

Extremist ideologies crystallize the often nebulous popular resentments toward Jews into vivid stereotypes. Cries of a
"Jewish Communist conspiracy" have long provided a focus
of such diatribes. Such charges command a facade of legitimacy because a disproportionate number of Argentine leftists, particularly Communists, have been Jewish (though they
represent a small minority of Jews and are ostracized by
major Jewish organizations). Although the great majority of
Jews traditionally have supported democratic and anti-Communist candidates such as former presidents Arturo Frondizi
and Arturo Illía, the scapegoating of all Jews as "Bolshevist
subversives" has continued.

Currently the *sine qua non* of anti-Semitic polemic is the
denunciation of "Zionist imperialism," an effective euphe-
mism in a land where most professed Jews are Zionist. The
Argentine who harbors prejudice against Jews yet wants to
consider himself tolerant and even idealistic (by the standards
of the "third world," with which Argentina tends to identify
itself) can excoriate Zionist machinations while denying anti-
Jewish feelings.

The crusade against the Zionist evil is by no means confined to extremists of the right. One thinks, for example, of

the 600 eminent intellectuals, Peronist leaders, and union officials from the head of the leftist Third World Priests, Carlos Mujica, to the conservative figure Matías Sánchez Sorondo, all of whom signed an advertisement in the *Journal Clarin* in 1971 denouncing the Jewish state as inherently usurping, racist, aggressive, and expansionist. One remembers, too, that despite the heralded liberalism of the civilian political parties a left Peronist deputy, Juan Carlos Cornejo Linares, created a stir in 1964 with a call for investigation of Zionist activity in Argentina. Linares thought it an open issue whether Zionism was menacing the nation's existence. The scholar Mauricio Dulfano notes that amidst the lively debate over Linares's proposal, a Jewish congressman introduced a motion to investigate the increase in anti-Semitic activity then deluging Argentina. His motion failed to muster a quorum for discussion. Like the left elsewhere in the world, the left in Argentina has not been much exercised by anti-Semitism.

Given the widespread contempt for Jews in Argentina, it is not surprising that extremists, often operating in a generally unstable social climate, have perpetrated anti-Semitic acts with little popular protest and scant government interference. These outrages date almost to the first organized Jewish settlements. The largely Slavic origins of these Jews enabled right-wing agitators to play upon the popular fear of "Russian revolutionaries." Sporadic incidents of gang violence culminated during the "Tragic Week" in January 1919, which left hundreds of Jews dead and thousands more injured. As the slaughter in the Jewish Quarter of Buenos Aires reached a crescendo, nearby police remained impassive. Sixty years later, the incident appears less an anomaly than an archetype for periodic explosions of anti-Semitic barbarism.

If civilian governments, like that in 1919, have proved too feeble or indifferent to check anti-Semitic acts, Argentina's numerous military regimes in this century have been inimical to Jewish welfare. In 1930, a military coup installed a group of German-trained officers whose xenophobia proved a more volatile fuel for bigotry than the anti-Marxist hysteria that had led to earlier tragedy. Government propagandists now cast the Jew as a subverter of the "national purpose," and throughout the decade right-wing police helped fascist gangs terrorize Jews with bombs, guns, and knives.

The military repression culminated in the early 1940s, when the ambitious army colonel and minister of Labor, Juan Domingo Perón, permitted the use of Jew-baiting tactics to enliven worker rallies. In a typical case of government-protected instigation, Peronist police beamed approval while hoodlums painted on a sidewalk in Buenos Aires, "Kill a Jew and be a patriot!" As Perón consolidated his power, the Jews were allowed a decade's respite from anti-Semitic persecution, to the extent that silent terror can be construed as an interlude. But in 1960, during the presidency of a liberal democrat, Arturo Frondizi, this precarious state of calm collapsed with the news that Israeli agents had seized mass murderer Adolf Eichmann in Buenos Aires. The event catalyzed an intense right-wing reaction by a lunatic fringe, which committed hundreds of anti-Semitic acts annually during the early 1960s. With exceptions, Argentine authorities divided—as one finds today as well—between those unable to restrain anti-Semitic criminals and those unwilling to. The latter element included key police officials, who routinely castigated Jewish victims of fascist attacks.

Jews who believed that their security had reached its nadir received an added shock in July 1966, when the democratic regime fell in a military coup. The new president, General Juan Carlos Onganía, intent upon suppressing left-wing elements, conducted a purge of civilian politicians that encompassed all Jewish officials, and he formed an inner circle of advisers that included a former Nazi collaborator and others inclined toward repressive measures.

The Onganía junta escalated its war against the Jews with the arbitrary arrest of Bernardo Jaroslavsky, a respected municipal official in Buenos Aires, followed by arrests of 18 Jewish business leaders, all eventually dismissed for lack of substantive charges. Anti-Semitic violence by largely unchecked private groups recurred throughout the rule of this and two successive juntas.

During the upsurge in left-wing guerrilla activity in the early 1970s, the worsening social conditions created a new focus of danger for the Jews: a host of rumors about Zionist intrigues. In Bahía Blanca, 420 miles from Buenos Aires, "international Zionism" was widely blamed for the death of Juan Perón's nationally revered wife, Eva (a victim of cancer in 1952). In two other major cities, Tucumán and Resistencia, public meetings condemned the "Zionist plot" to undermine Argentine nationality.

The military's restoration of civilian politics in 1973, under intense popular pressure, merely sharpened the ambivalence of the Jewish position in Argentina. Septuagenarian Juan Perón returned from exile to regain the presidency, while retaining his political North Star of expediency toward the "Jewish questions." He denied that his Justicialista party was anti-Semitic, yet cultivated ties with anti-Semites in and outside of Parliament. He appointed José Ber Gelbard as minister of finance, yet tacitly approved a public accusation by one of his closest aides that the presence of Jews in government was impeding the national interest, which dictated closer ties to oil-rich Arab states. Amid these conflicting signals, anti-Semitic acts increased, a trend exacerbated by a collapsing economy, rising guerrilla activity on both left and right, and the declaration of a "State of Siege" in 1975 by Perón's widow and successor, Isabel, which moved the nation further toward authoritarianism.

When the military swept away the vestiges of democracy by deposing Isabel Perón in 1976, in order to suppress insurrection more efficiently, the position of Argentina's Jews deteriorated. In the junta's zeal to eliminate suspected left-wing dissidents, it awarded fascist groups free rein to eliminate "undesirables." Soon self-appointed death squads were roaming the country with impunity, murdering prominent liberals, trade unionists, intellectuals, and Jews of every occupational and political background. These activities were flanked by a proliferation of Nazi writings selling briskly on Argentine newsstands. Very popular in 1976 was a new edition of *Mein Kampf*.

The number of anti-Semitic attacks has diminished somewhat in recent years, but the active partnership among fascists in and out of government remains vigorous. What can be done to reduce the danger to Argentina's Jewish community? Some, including Jacobo Timerman, believe that unless people and governments everywhere protest anti-Semitic actions (and indeed all violations of human rights), these evils will spread in a moral vacuum. But others, including some Argentine and American Jewish officials, fear that such protest, however morally cathartic, might provoke the military junta into further acts of repression. Unlike the equally debated question of whether anti-Semitism in Argentina even exists, it is a complex issue that admits no certain prediction. Yet if history is any guide, concerted opposition to Argentine anti-Semitism is likely to bring salutary results, though more limited than many advocates of protest contend.

American diplomatic pressure appears to have contributed, though no one knows just how significantly, to greater restraint by earlier Argentine military governments. In 1943, for example, Minister of Justice Martínez Zuviría, a notorious anti-Semite, banned Yiddish journals (on the ground that the censor could not read them), and issued rulings that virtually prohibited kosher meat processing in the capital. After pressure from the United States government, including a sharp public statement about repression from President Franklin Roosevelt, these laws were abruptly reversed.

Again, in 1966, when anti-Semitic terror was at one of its many peaks, demonstrations at the United Nations and strong protests by President Lyndon Johnson and other political notables such as Senator Robert Kennedy of New York were followed by conciliatory gestures from President Onganía. He implicitly denied anti-Semitic intent, and even continued a tradition of Argentina's civilian presidents by sending public greetings to the Jewish community on its high holy days.

American pressure on the current junta has also had some positive effect on the plight of Argentine Jews, though how much (and with what complications for diplomatic relations generally) may be disputed. According to Jacobo Timerman, the intercession of Patricia Derian, President Carter's assistant secretary of state for human rights and humanitarian affairs, saved him from execution. It appears that outside pressure also has encouraged some elements within the junta to try to moderate the fervor with which their colleagues have pursued Zionists and other suspected "subversives."

Actions by the Jewish community itself—despite its difficult position—at different times have helped to fight persecution. In the early 1940s, there were episodes of successful armed Jewish resistance to marauding Nazi bands in Buenos Aires. In 1962 (under a civilian government) a Jewish-organized demonstration to protest police indifference to the torture of a 19-year-old Jewish girl gained the active support of some non-Jews as well as Jews.

One must qualify any optimism drawn from these events, which are, after all, limited victories in a generally dismal context. Still, if vigilance toward anti-Semitism in Argentina, including public pronouncements as well as private diplomacy, cannot eliminate this anti-social malady, it may at least help check potential tragedies to come. But even this kind of vigilance requires a more sustained concern, commitment, and simple awareness than world opinion has thus far shown. Further, as the current repressive situation possibly takes a few tentative steps for the better, the strong temptation will arise, as in previous decades, to dismiss anti-Semitic horrors as an ugly but aberrant relic of Argentine history. Those with a sense of what that history has meant for Argentina's Jews, however, realize that such "aberrations" are all too likely to haunt them again.

A CRACKDOWN ON RIGHTS[6]

In Geneva last month, Argentine human-rights activist Emilio Mignone presented a harsh case against his own country. Appearing before the United Nations Commission on

[6] Reprint of article by John Brecher, staff reporter. *Newsweek.* 97:47. Mr. 16 '81. Copyright 1981, by Newsweek, Inc. All Rights Reserved. Reprinted by Permission.

Human Rights, Mignone charged that 6,000 men and women seized by Argentine security agents in the past six years had never been heard from again. He supported those charges with documents painstakingly compiled by his Center for Legal and Social Studies in Buenos Aires. Then Mignone went home. A few days later plainclothes police burst into the center and seized the list of *desaparecidos* (vanished ones). Then they raided the homes of the center's leaders and arrested six of them—including Emilio Mignone.

Late last week the activists were released after the judge reviewing their case declared that it would be "unfair" to hold them indefinitely. But the charges against them were not dropped. The government had hinted darkly that the six somehow had violated national-security laws, perhaps by stealing top-secret maps and documents. In fact, all six activists are well known to be nonpolitical; they have fought their human-rights battle in the courts, not in the streets. Mignone, a lawyer and a former Under Secretary of Education, founded the center after his own daughter disappeared in 1976. Another detainee, José Federico Westerkamp, is one of the country's top scientists—he helped to research the laser—whose son has been in jail for nearly six years without formal charges. In Argentina, Mignone and Westerkamp are at least as well known for their human-rights efforts as Adolfo Pérez Esquivel, who won the Nobel Peace Prize last year—and marched last week to protest their arrest.

Until the crackdown on Mignone and his fellow activists, the Argentine Government had been easing up on dissidents, partly because of Jimmy Carter's human-rights campaign. Then came the election of Ronald Reagan—and a different American stance toward repressive regimes. For example, the Reagan State Department lifted sanctions imposed by Carter when Chile refused to extradite three agents indicted by a U.S. grand jury for plotting the 1976 murder of Orlando Letelier in Washington. In Geneva, the Administration voted to terminate a U.N. inquiry into abuses within Chile. And there were reports that the U.S. delegation had been instructed to vote against continuing investigation of Argentina. That issue was circumvented by a compromise.

Gesture: When Mignone was arrested, the Administration contented itself with the observation that "no useful purpose can be served by public condemnation." It was not clear why Washington seemed so solicitous. Argentina is not a strategic ally, and is militantly nonaligned. It refused, for example, to go along with the U.S. embargo on grain shipments to the Soviet Union, receiving in turn Moscow's support on the human-rights issue. The Administration may be trying to make a gesture to Gen. Roberto Viola, who will take over as President later this month. Human-rights activists also have high hopes for Viola, who plans the first civilian-dominated Cabinet since 1976. The most optimistic view of last week's raids was that the current regime wanted to destroy the list of *desaparecidos* before Viola could use it to prosecute right-wing kidnappers.

THE UN HUMAN RIGHTS COMMISSION[7]

The sky over Geneva was overcast during most of February, although, people say, a few miles away, up in the mountains, the sky was brilliant blue and the snow-white peaks shone in the sun. Under this overcast, out of the sun, there met this year again, for the 37th time, the UN Human Rights Commission. Each year, for six weeks, representatives of 43 nations sit, like 43 judges, surveying a prepared agenda on human rights in various nations of the world.

Geneva is the most expensive city in the world. It teems with diplomats, experts, technicians, and their families, who arrive with the hard-earned currencies of many governments.

[7] Reprint of magazine article entitled "Winter before Spring," by Michael Novak, chief U.S. delegate to the United Nations Commission on Human Rights and resident scholar in religion and public policy at the American Enterprise Institute for Public Policy Research. *National Review.* 33:494. My 1, '81. © 1981, National Review, Inc. Reprinted by permission.

Taxi-drivers and restaurateurs, secretaries and shopkeepers, travel services and waiters work around the clock to separate them from their francs. They succeed quite quickly and without pause.

The second thing one notices is security. One is taught to assume that telephones are tapped, that discussions in certain locations ought to be avoided, that with certain persons one ought to be on special guard. Terrorists are of constant concern to diplomats. Here in neutral Switzerland, I have remembered images of our Pilgrim fathers walking to church with rifles over their shoulders. Here the stark, stubby submachine gun fits neatly under the arm.

The Puppets Exit

What have we, then? Cold war? Detente? Or something significantly different and far more dangerous than either?

At our sessions, the Soviet Union and China called each other liars in the high pungency of Leninist invective. Each time the representatives of Democratic Kampuchea [Cambodia] spoke (often enough to produce comedy) the Soviets and their satellites, including Cuba, as if uplifted by a heavenly puppeteer, jerked out of their seats and exited together. This evoked mirth from all who only sat and served.

Syria heaped insults on Egypt, and Egypt retaliated. The observer of the Arab League pleaded for Arab brotherhood, then went on longer than brotherhood would commend to kick Egypt once or twice himself. Libya attacked Morocco, whose delegate had replied with malicious wit to Algeria. Sad observers from Chad and Afghanistan arose to say that their nations have not been invaded, only assisted by kindly big brothers.

The quality of rhetoric was not always easy to believe, even as one heard it. Zionism, defined by the UN since 1975 as racism, is now described as the main source of antisemitism. Profits are invariably described as "obscene." (So far at least, no one has spoken of losses as chaste.) Cuba attacks Chile and El Salvador with rhetoric matched to its armed subversions.

The Soviet delegation—led by Valerian Zorin, an amiable, child-faced, white-haired man of eighty, who presided over events in Prague in 1948—has advantages which Western delegations lack. To gain credibility, his researchers have him cite Western publications such as the *Philadelphia Inquirer, Time,* and the *Washington Post.* (Westerners can hardly quote TASS.)

The Soviets work full time, having speeches written well in advance (*long* speeches), full of attacks upon their chief targets of the moment, not only for themselves but for their satellites. When Bulgaria speaks, the voice is Moscow's. When Byelorussia speaks, the voice is Moscow's. When Cuba speaks, the voice is Moscow's. They attack every item on the agenda with at least eight unanimous delegations.

Given their own record on human rights, it is one of the wonders of the world that the Soviets sit in the seats of the judges. One longs to see Aleksandr Solzhenitsyn enter this room. One longs to hear him count the roll of the 65 million citizens killed by Lenin and Stalin, as he does in *The Gulag Archipelago.*

I told one Western delegate, at a reception, that I would in future read the absurdist drama of Ionesco with greater appreciation. He didn't quite catch me, for he said: "UNESCO is even worse!"

Yet, individually, most of the delegates to Geneva are fine people. In the informal moments, one truly enjoys their company. But arguments over human rights, once they have been politicized as here they are, are not like any other political arguments. Human rights are of the spirit. They depend entirely upon the truth. Lies destroy human rights far more effectively than assassins or bomb-throwers. Lies degrade the language, and despoil the intellectual premises, of human rights. They poison the due process of human rights.

Fingers on the Windpipe

Some of our allies assured me that these exercises are essentially harmless, mere propaganda, nothing but rhetoric. But the circle of usable language grows ever smaller. The darkness of Orwellian doublespeak swirls over precious achievements of the human spirit. Human rights as we understand them are not yet strangled to death, but cold fingers are on their windpipe.

Yet human rights do offer the right place to stand and fight. The Declaration of Human Rights is—one of our allies put it eloquently—like a snapshot of the values of the West in 1949 at their high point in history. The whole world, although understanding the basic concepts in other languages and other cultural frameworks, is now using our own most cherished words. It is our job to speak those words as we understand them. We must argue our case, persuade, lobby, and show every political skill required for successful technical work in a commission such as this.

The contest for the future, Solzhenitsyn says, is radically a contestation of the human spirit. It is on the battleground of the spirit that the contest will be decided. The battleground of human rights is most favorable to all that we care for. In this particular overcast valley, we must do our utmost.

III. HUMAN RIGHTS AND U.S. FOREIGN POLICY

EDITOR'S INTRODUCTION

This final section examines from many differing points of view the extent to which human rights should be a factor in the making of U.S. foreign policy. In the first article, Warren Christopher, former Deputy Secretary of State under President Carter, contends that "A firm emphasis on human rights is . . . a pragmatic, tough-minded policy. Our human rights policy serves not just the ideals but the interests of the United States."

In the second article, *Nation's Business* asks "Should we export morality?"—should U.S. businesses restrict trading with countries that violate human rights? Next, in a *U.S. News & World Report* double interview Jeane Kirkpatrick, U.S. Ambassador to the United Nations, argues that "The central goal of our foreign policy is not the moral elevation of other nations," while Patricia M. Derian, former assistant secretary of state for human rights counters that the Carter policy was in line with international law and saved human lives. The *New Yorker* also takes issue with the Reagan Administration's de-emphasis of human rights claiming that "Our foreign policy then becomes nothing more than a military shield, containing no reflection of the spirit of our country."

The sharp contrast in the varying perspectives on human rights is shown in the next several articles. The transcript of the televised *MacNeil-Lehrer Report* highlights the differences between the Carter and the Reagan approaches to human rights. Two articles from the *Wall Street Journal* and the *New Republic* examine the current emphasis on human rights violations by totalitarian governments as opposed to those by authoritarian governments.

The next selection by William F. Buckley, Jr., writing in *National Review,* analyzes favorably a speech on human rights and national policy made by Ambassador Kirkpatrick.

"The Reagan Administration has lost little time in directing U.S. foreign policy away from what it sees as a misplaced emphasis on human rights," claims the next article from *America*.

Excerpts from four addresses before the UN Commission on Human Rights by the chief U.S. delegate, Michael Novak, are given next. The topics include anti-Semitism, terrorism, self-determination, and the right to development.

Writing in the *New Republic*, Stephen Cohen, a former Deputy Assistant Secretary of State for Human Rights under Carter, points out that "before the Reagan Administration consigns the human rights policy to the diplomatic scrap heap, it will have to contend with a pro-human rights bipartisan coalition on the House Foreign Affairs Committee."

This viewpoint is echoed in the next selection from *Christian Century* referring to the withdrawal of Reagan's original nominee to the human rights post. ". . . It was a congressional committee that told a popular president that respect for human rights is still central to the American vision."

The final article criticizes the moralistic Carter approach to human rights as "righteous rhetoric of a fundamentalist sermon," but at the same time disagrees with the Reagan Administration attitude that the U.S. "cannot afford the luxury of being the moral policeman of the world, imposing its own values." The author concludes that "The quest for human rights and human dignity is a phenomenon of contemporary life of universal dimensions and immense significance in the struggle between East and West. And those who do not grasp its significance do not know much about the world we live in and the forces that shape it."

HUMAN RIGHTS AND THE NATIONAL INTEREST[1]

Three and a half years ago, President Carter introduced into our foreign policy a theme both old and new: old, be-

[1] Reprint of statement by Deputy Secretary Warren M. Christopher before the American Bar Association, Honolulu, August 4, 1980. (Current Policy no 206) United States. Department of State. Bureau of Public Affairs. Office of Public Communications. Washington, DC 20520. '80.

cause it arose from our most basic national values; new in the sharp emphasis the President gave it. I am referring, of course, to human rights. "Because we are free," the President said in his inaugural address, "we can never be indifferent to the fate of freedom elsewhere."

From the beginning, the President was determined that American foreign policy should give active, explicit support to three categories of human rights:

☐ The right to be free from violations of personal integrity— torture, arbitrary arrest or imprisonment, and violations of due process;
☐ The right to fulfill vital economic needs, such as food, shelter, health care, and education; and
☐ Civil and political rights—freedom of thought, expression, assembly, travel, and participation in government.

I need not remind this audience that our commitment to human rights rests upon a large and growing body of law. Domestically, human rights legislation enacted by our Congress makes clear that our commitment is truly a national commitment—and that it is here to stay. Internationally, the human rights conventions, the Universal Declaration of Human Rights, and other basic documents make clear that the values we are seeking to advance are truly global values. I am proud that the ABA [American Bar Association] and the Carter Administration are united in supporting Senate ratification of the human rights conventions. And I am hopeful that our mutual efforts to achieve ratification will soon be successful.

In the 3½ years since President Carter proclaimed his policy, we have made real progress. We have effectively institutionalized human rights as a major element of U.S. foreign policy. A Bureau of Human Rights and Humanitarian Affairs has been established by statute, headed by an Assistant Secretary of State. Every American Ambassador has been instructed to report regularly on human rights conditions in the country to which he or she is posted. And the State Department's annual country reports on human rights have become one of the most important and objective sources of information on human rights conditions around the world.

Even more importantly, human rights has been placed squarely on the diplomatic table. The subject has become an item of serious discussion between us and the nations with which we deal—a dramatic change from past diplomatic practice. We have worked to strengthen the human rights efforts of international bodies like the United Nations and the Inter-American Human Rights Commission. And human rights performance has become one of the key criteria we use in apportioning American aid to other nations.

This new emphasis in our foreign policy has not come without controversy. There has been vigorous criticism of our human rights policy on the ground that it smacks of a fuzzy-headed idealism, that it is unrelated to the pursuit of our basic national interests. Some critics have suggested that human rights are a millstone around the neck of U.S. foreign policy; that it has injected into our diplomacy an interventionist element that can only weaken our position in the world and even destabilize other governments.

After 3½ years of deep involvement in human rights issues, I am more convinced than ever that this point of view is simply and starkly wrong. I will go further: To abandon the pursuit of human rights would gravely damage not only the hopes of millions abroad but also the foreign policy and long-term security of the United States.

A firm emphasis on human rights is not an alternative to "realpolitik," nor is it simply a side issue in our foreign policy. It is, instead, a central part of a pragmatic, tough-minded policy. Our human rights policy serves not just the ideals but the interests of the United States.

Let me support that assertion by discussing four of the ways in which our stress on human rights serves important interests of our nation.

Peace and Stability

First, our human rights policy directly serves our long-term interest in peace and stability.

There is, perhaps, a natural temptation to equate stability with the status quo. Yet experience has demonstrated that the opposite is often true. The silence of official repression may appear to be "stability"—but it is often far more fragile than it appears. The misleading quiet of repression has too often turned out to be the calm before a violent, revolutionary storm. In such storms of violence, American interests are often damaged—and targets of opportunity are created for the Soviet Union or other forces hostile to the United States.

Governments that respect the rights of their people, and which reflect the will of their people, are far less vulnerable to such disruptions. As the *Washington Post* suggested just a few days ago, critics of the Carter Administration's human rights policy sometimes overlook the fact that democracy can be the "shock absorber" for change in developing countries. "Democracy," the *Post* said, "offers a process of consent and accommodation—and dignity—to societies undergoing racking change."

By advancing human rights, we help to alleviate the sources of tension and instability before they erupt into violence, before our interests are harmed.

Our human rights policy is, thus, a vital element of our effort to align the United States with support for peaceful, constructive change. We are not so naive as to equate all change with progress—for that equation makes no more sense than equating stability and the status quo. But we recognize that the suppression of peaceful change often makes violence and terror inevitable.

That is what Vice President Mondale had in mind 2 weeks ago when he warned, on a visit to Africa, that "the clock is ticking in South Africa"—that it is important to support peaceful change in the interest of avoiding violent upheaval there.

There is, in other words, a direct connection between support for human rights and the prospects for peace. And so in the Middle East, our emphasis is on a comprehensive peace settlement: A stable peace in that troubled region requires that we find a mechanism to assure the right of Palestinians to participate in determining their own future, while at the

same time assuring the right of Israelis to live within secure
borders.

In Central America, our human rights policy seeks to
strengthen the democratic center and to support those who
want to build stable and pluralistic societies.

☐ In Nicaragua, for example, decades of corrupt, oppressive
rule finally led virtually the entire country to demand change.
We could not have stemmed that tide of change even if we
had wished to do so. What we can do, and what we are trying
to do, is to encourage those forces in Nicaragua who want to
insure that change moves in a free and democratic direction.
We know our help cannot guarantee success. But our refusal
to help would almost certainly guarantee defeat. And it
would ease the way for those who advocate "a Cuban solution" in Nicaragua.
☐ In El Savador, violence from both left and right is abusing
the Salvadoran people and threatening a moderate, reformist
government. If that moderate government fails, the most
likely outcome is full-scale civil war. We are supporting that
government and its reforms to avoid just such an outcome.

All should recognize that American support for democratic change in struggling Third World countries is complex
and risky and involves difficult judgments. But the alternatives are riskier still, both for our values and for our security
interests.

Our support of constructive change serves to deny the Soviets tempting targets of opportunity. Consider our experience in Rhodesia—now the new nation of Zimbabwe. The
decision of our government to maintain sanctions against
Rhodesia, and to support a negotiated settlement of the racial
strife there, was controversial. It was difficult to sustain in this
country and in the Congress. But it has borne hopeful fruit.

Zimbabwe was born through a democratic election. The
Soviets' hope to exploit conflict has been frustrated. Western
influence has been preserved.

There is, as I have said, an economic dimension to our

support for human rights. Some of the most dangerous sources of instability in the world are economic. Such instability is bad for our security interests, and it is bad for American business, too. Respect for human rights creates an atmosphere of stability in which business and investment can flourish.

Foreign assistance is one of the most effective tools for coping with these economic sources of instability. Today, unfortunately, our foreign assistance is too meager to serve adequately our own humanitarian, economic, or security interests. But we try to target such aid as we can provide to narrow income disparities, to help people directly, and thus to ease social tensions in developing countries. We also channel our aid increasingly to countries that respect human rights, to countries that are trying to preserve representative government or to move from dictatorship to democracy.

This channeling of our aid is sometimes attacked as "intervention." We are admonished that other governments have a right to choose their own practices and forms of governments. Of course they do. But we have the right, and the obligation, to choose which governments and practices we will support with our scarce dollars.

Our resources and our powers are limited. But by working to ease grinding poverty, by supporting peaceful, constructive change, we believe we serve the cause of real peace and stability in the world. And this is very much in our national interest.

U.S. Security

The second point I wish to emphasize is that the United States will be more secure in a world where more governments respect the rights of their people—because countries that respect human rights make stronger allies and better friends.

This reality is illustrated by the democracies in Western Europe, in the Andean Pact in South America, in Japan and in the ASEAN [Association of South East Asian Nations] group in Southeast Asia. Their commitment to human rights gives them an inner strength and stability that enables them to stand steadfastly with us on the most difficult security issues of our time. By seeking to widen the circle of such countries, our human rights policy directly enhances our security interests.

Unfortunately, of course, not all our friends and allies can meet this high standard. One of the greatest challenges we will face in future years is the challenge of meshing our security assistance with human rights persuasion: combining military assistance to those who need it with strong encouragement to undertake the kind of internal reform necessary for long-term stability.

We face this challenge in our dealing with allies like South Korea and the Philippines—nations whose friendship is important to our security, nations whose governments we are trying to influence on human rights issues. Our security assistance to such countries supports a basic human right—the right of their people to live in safety from external attack. At the same time, by encouraging their governments to undertake internal reforms that will improve life for their people, we serve their long-term security interests and our own.

U.S. Influence

Third, support for human rights enhances the influence of the United States in important world arenas.

Too often in the past, the United States has allowed itself to be portrayed as a complacent, status quo power, insensitive to the quest of others for the freedoms we enjoy. And the result has often weakened the influence of the United States.

Our human rights policy counters that tendency. It identifies the United States with leaders around the world who are trying to improve the lot of their people.

We stand at a moment in history when widening literacy, mass communications, and urbanization have produced a global political awakening. This is a fundamental event in human history that expresses itself, above all, in the intensified demand for human rights. And our response to that demand has meant a new influence and goodwill for our country.

The respect for the people of Panama which motivated the Panama Canal treaties has in turn earned us a new and continuing respect throughout Latin America. The settlement in Zimbabwe has had positive effects on our relations with African and other developing countries. Our recent success in increasing trade with Third World nations can be laid in part to the growing trust generated by our human rights record.

So, too, our ability to offer leadership at the forthcoming Madrid Conference on Security and Cooperation in Europe will benefit from our human rights policy. We will go to the table at Madrid with a solid record of commitment to human rights.

In essence, our support for human rights gives us a way of emphasizing what we are for, not simply what we oppose. It gives us a way of taking the ideological initiative, instead of merely reacting. It gives us a rubric under which to organize our support for due process, economic progress, and democratic principles.

In the competition between the Soviet Union and ourselves, we benefit enormously from the comparison between our values and political methods and those of the Soviets. We pursue human rights for their own sake and would do so even if there were no Soviet Union. But there can be no doubt that our human rights policy does confound our adversaries.

The Soviets fear our human rights policy because their own human rights record is so abysmal and because they sense the power that the ideas of freedom and human dignity exert. Georgi Vladimov, a Soviet author and dissident, recently commented on U.S. human rights policy. "I don't know if President Carter will enter American history," he said, "but he has already entered Russian history with this policy."

Surely no recent event is more damaging to Soviet pretensions than their aggression in Afghanistan. It is important to remember—and to remind the world—that the continuing

Soviet assault upon Afghanistan is a human rights issue. We oppose the Soviet presence there not only because of our strategic concerns but also because the Afghan people are being brutalized in a war of subjugation and repression. Whole villages are being wiped out; mosques are being shot up; there is mounting evidence that chemical warfare is being waged by the Soviets against the Afghan people. The 1 million refugees who have fled the country attest to the dire plight of the Afghan people.

The influence and goodwill we gain by standing up for human rights cannot always be tangibly measured, but it is real. Our Embassy reports, our conversations with foreign diplomats, and the foreign press show that U.S. foreign policy is widely perceived as clearly and courageously supporting human rights. We need more, not less, of this positive policy.

Refugee Problem

Fourth, our support for human rights may offer the only long-term solution to one of the most pressing problems on the international agenda—the problem of refugees.

We live in an epoch of refugees. More than 15 million people have fled their homes in recent years because of wars, civil disturbances, persecution, hostile government policies, or other local conditions. Vietnamese, Kampucheans, Afghans, and now Cubans have fled from conditions which, for a variety of reasons, they found intolerable.

In the short term, we must seek to ease the misery of these innocent people. And we have done so. We have served as a haven for large numbers of refugees from around the world; and we have provided massive quantities of humanitarian relief. I am proud of America's response.

Ultimately, however, the solution lies not simply in arrangements to ease the plight of refugees; it lies in efforts to end the misery and repression that caused them to flee in the first place.

When a government respects the human rights of its citizens, refugees are a rare phenomenon. And we know that refugees are more likely to return home when the human rights situation has improved at home. In the last year, for example, the end of warfare in Nicaragua and Zimbabwe has enabled large numbers of refugees from these countries to return to their homes.

Global Progress

As we look back over the past 3½ years, we can see that the United States is identified more clearly than ever as a beacon of support for human rights. Worldwide publicity and concern for human rights have increased dramatically.

And we can see encouraging progress in many parts of the world.

☐ In Africa: Nigeria, Upper Volta, and Ghana have become democracies. Niger and Togo are expanding civilian participation in government. Dictators have fallen in Uganda, the Central African Republic, and Equatorial Guinea.

☐ In Latin America, there have been some heartening developments. Just last week, Peru returned to democracy with the inauguration of its first elected President in more than 10 years; and Honduras returned to full constitutionality. There have been setbacks, too, like the recent brutal coup in Bolivia. But in a number of countries throughout the hemisphere, democratic processes are being reaffirmed in the face of heavy pressure; and where there is back-sliding—as in Bolivia—those responsible are subjected to an unprecedented wave of condemnation by those nations that care.

☐ In Morocco, Bangladesh, the Sudan, Indonesia, Nepal, and Paraguay, significant numbers of political prisoners have been released.

☐ In Thailand, freedom of the press has been established and the rights of political parties have been broadened. And in South Asia, Sri Lanka, with a good human rights record of its own, has become a regional center of human rights activity.

☐ And equally important, for the long run, human rights institutions are active as never before. The U.N. Human Rights

Commission has become more vigorous and energetic. The Inter-American Human Rights Court held its first meeting last year, and the Inter-American Commission on Human Rights—which has been active since the 1960s—continues a full schedule of country visits and reviews of complaints filed by victims and their supporters. The Organization of African Unity is now in the process of setting up its own regular Human Rights Commission. Slowly but steadily, these institutions are growing as an important force for the promotion of human rights.

The United States does not take credit for these events. But we do buttress them with moral and material support. And we can take satisfaction that our policies and our leadership are now visibly in accord with the aspirations of millions of the world's people. The real point is that the human rights policy is not ours alone. Let me quote the opening sentence from the inaugural address last week of Peru's new President: "Constitutional order, human rights, and freedom of the press are hereby reestablished by the will of the people."

Our efforts to express our deepest values through our human rights policy are working. They give us a glimpse of something we see all too seldom in the world: a happy situation in which American interests and American ideals converge.

THE WRONGS OF THE RIGHTS POLICY[2]

As the U.S. trade deficit continues to grow, the need for more exports becomes increasingly obvious. Government restrictions such as the Foreign Corrupt Practices Act and curbs on trading with countries that violate human rights are among factors standing in the way of an improvement in our export performance.

[2] Reprint of staff-written article. *Nation's Business.* 68:52. 0. '80. Reprinted by permission from Nation's Business, October, 1980. Copyright 1980 by Nation's Business, Chamber of Commerce of the United States.

Nation's Business asked readers in the August Sound Off: "Should we export morality?" The vote was no, by a margin of 4 to 1.

"Our CEO recently observed that U.S. morality has become a major U.S. export and described it as an exercise in futility," says Peter Bush, director of public relations for the Boeing Company, Seattle, Wash. "Unilateral pressure of this kind seldom has any effect except the loss of markets and American jobs to our foreign competitors. Our company has lost sales involving hundreds of millions of dollars because of this unilateral U.S. export disincentive."

Robert R. Briggs, president of One Way Industrial Supply, Inc., Boleta, Calif., disagrees. What better export, he asks, is there than morality? "If we fail to stand up for those ideals which make our country unique among nations, then we have little to offer the world. As a proud American, I am thankful for the rights which I enjoy in this country. I do not wish to do business with those who deny others those basic rights. If this means economic loss, so be it."

Those on the negative side feel the marketplace, and not moral standards imposed by government, should dictate regulations on trade. "The purpose of business in our capitalist society is to make a profit through competition in the marketplace. The marketplace sets the rules. Let our businesses export products for profit, if they can, according to the local ground rules," says D. L. Wackerhagen, vice president of Security Forces, Inc., Charlotte, N.C.

Lloyd W. Frueh, president of Bartley & Lloyd Corporation, Rocky River, Ohio, agrees: "We should be free to do business in foreign countries without trying to force our moral standards and customs on people of other nations. The resentment created far outweighs any possible benefits. Let us go out and get the business competitively, thereby strengthening the dollar and regaining the position and power we previously enjoyed."

"Most economists I know, and I am among them, are free traders," says John V. Terry, corporate consultant for industrial and public affairs at the Allen Canning Company, Inc., Siloam Springs, Ark. "There is an old saying that you can cut off your nose to spite your face. This is essentially what we do when we try to punish other nations by not trading with them on pseudomoral grounds."

On the other hand, Freeda Hodges, co-owner of Hodges Pest Control, O'Fallon, Mo., says: "As long as our nation believes in human rights, we should stand up for them whenever it is necessary. Anything worthwhile can be expected to cost us in some way. The question is, are we willing to pay the price?"

And Glenn C. Hawks, vice president for PRC Toups, Ventura, Calif., says: "The U.S. has continually slipped from the pedestal of leadership we enjoyed for several decades. If we allow our stand on human rights to go as well, then what do we stand for?"

But Bernard Huntebrinker, Jr., vice president of Toledo Lithograin & Plate Company, Toledo, Ohio, thinks we shouldn't try to export morality because "it is a concept that is constantly being changed. Whether it is religion or politics, there are too many definitions within this country, and those ideals are not always the best for others. If it is not possible to export a consistent concept, we should export no concept at all."

Furthermore, Dick Jokinen, assistant administrator for the Country Manor Nursing Home in Sartell, Minn., says: "Morality cannot be mandated or regulated; it is taught and passed on by example to those to whom it has appeal. Thus it is ludicrous to base our trade potential upon various interpretations of accepted morals."

Many who oppose restricting trade for morality reasons criticize the U.S. for lack of morality at home. "We cannot afford to export morality; we have so little that it is a scarce commodity!" says Jack Wiziarde, president of Elgin Diamond Products Company, Elgin, Ill. S.S. Steele, chief executive officer of S.S. Steele & Company, Inc., Mobile, Ala., says: "If you mean should we export the morality we possess, such as our pervasive drug culture, our increasingly high crime rate, our lack of respect for the laws by all segments of our society including law enforcement agencies, our me-first philosophy and so forth, then obviously the answer must be negative."

"Other countries have political philosophies different from ours and, especially in underdeveloped countries, there is no way that our political system will work for them," argues Walt Hohnbaum, vice president of Camos & Hohnbaum, Inc. in Lenexa, Kans.

Bruno Tafani, owner of Bruno General Contracting, Forty Fort, Pa., takes the affirmative side. He says: "Human life seems to be almost valueless lately. If trade restriction is the only language people will listen to in regard to human life, then I say let's export morality."

OVERHAUL U.S. POLICY ON HUMAN RIGHTS?[3]

Interview With Jeane Kirkpatrick
U.S. Ambassador to the United Nations

Q Ambassador Kirkpatrick, the crisis in El Salvador raises the question of how the U.S. should deal with human-rights violations. Why do you favor discarding the Carter administration's approach abroad?

A Because it was utopian, because it was conducted outside of the political and historical context, and because it didn't work. It used a concept of human rights that was far too broad. It included not only legal and personal rights, such as freedom from arbitrary arrest and torture and a guarantee of due process, and a full range of democratic political rights, such as freedom of speech, press, assembly, elections, but also a full range of economic rights—the right to food, shelter, education, medical care—which amounted to the demand that all countries become affluent social democracies.

[3]Reprint of interview with Jeane Kirkpatrick, U.S. Ambassador to the United Nations. *U.S. News & World Report.* 90:49–50. Mr. 2, '81.

Q You see that as an unrealistic standard?
A Yes. That is a standard which virtually no country in
the world can meet. Some people think Sweden or Denmark
might. West Germany and France don't. We ourselves don't.
And when you set up a standard that no real country meets,
you end up with no standard at all and you operate, instead,
on the basis of arbitrary judgments.

So arbitrariness became, along with utopianism, a leading
characteristic of the Carter policy. It became a policy of
being *selectively* unfriendly to autocracies. Moreover, it encouraged us to wrap ourselves in a mantle of righteousness
while pursuing hypocritical policies.

*Q You said the Carter administration ignored the political
context of rights issues—*
A It measured all countries by the same standards—disre-
garding differences in history, political traditions and social
conditions. If, for example, a country was combatting dissidents, no account was taken of whether that country had a
tradition of democracy and due process, or had ever been
anything but autocratic; of whether it was miserably poor or
had an affluent economy; of the fact that it might be in the
midst of a civil war or under guerrilla attack. Political thinking that takes no account of the concrete circumstances and
traditions and values of a people not only is useless but
usually turns out to be damaging.

Q Specifically, what damage did it do?
A By helping to destabilize the Somoza regime in Nicaragua, for example, it fanned the flames of a civil war in which
some 40,000 Nicaraguans lost their most basic human right—
the right to life. Another 100,000 were left homeless, and
some 2 billion dollars' worth of destruction was wrought. A
Sandinista regime was ushered in which instituted measures
more repressive than those of Somoza. Similar mistakes were
made in El Salvador, Guatemala and Bolivia.

Our position in the Western Hemisphere has deteriorated
to the point where we must now defend ourselves against the
threat of a ring of Soviet bases being established on and
around our borders. I'm not saying that the Carter human-
rights policy was the only factor in bringing this about, but it

certainly played a role. One reason for the failure of the Carter policy was the belief that you can influence governments and people more effectively by hitting them over the head with a two-by-four, excoriating and humiliating them publicly and treating them like moral pariahs than by using quiet persuasion and diplomacy.

Q Defenders of the Carter approach argue that it resulted in an improvement of conditions in Argentina and Chile—

A To think that such improvements were the result of our policy is a good example of the arrogance of power, of a colossal overestimation of our influence. In both of these countries, as well as in Brazil and other Latin American countries, there is a long tradition of swings between military dictatorship and constitutionalism. It is this and not our policy that explains the current movement in these countries toward a return to government by law.

Q Didn't the Carter policy help some individuals?

A It did. But, by and large, it failed in its goal of leaving more people more free and better off than they were. During the Carter years, the boundaries of freedom were constricted in as many places as they were expanded.

The principal function of the policy has been to make us feel good about ourselves. But that is not an appropriate foreign-policy goal.

Q Will the new administration turn its back on human rights?

A Absolutely not. But our approach will be different.

First, the concrete circumstances in which a human-rights violation takes place will be taken into account. Take El Salvador. It is engulfed in civil war, and I know of no country which has ever successfully carried out reforms while fighting a civil war. Besides, Napoleón Duarte, the junta leader, is and has always been known as a social reformer. The junta *is* a reform government. But as to how and when to carry out these reforms, I'd rather trust his judgment than yours or mine or that of our government.

Or take Africa. It is filled with moderately repressive autocracies—governments headed by military men who came to power by military coup. Does anyone seriously believe we should therefore not have relations with those governments?

We're not free to have relations only with the democratic countries of this world. And in governments, as in life, there are degrees of evil. To say that measles is less bad than meningitis doesn't make you pro-measles, does it?

Q Where will the Reagan administration draw the line?

A Speaking generally, we must make it perfectly clear that we are revolted by torture and can never feel spiritual kinship with a government that engages in torture. But the central goal of our foreign policy should be not the moral elevation of other nations, but the preservation of a civilized conception of our own national self-interest.

Copyright 1981, U.S. News & World Report, Inc.

OVERHAUL U.S. POLICY ON HUMAN RIGHTS?[4]

Interview With Patricia M. Derian
Former Assistant Secretary of State for Human Rights

Q Ms. Derian, why do you oppose abandonment of the Carter approach to human rights abroad?

A I oppose it for three good reasons. First, the Carter approach is in our long-range national interest. Second, we must conduct our foreign policy in a way consistent with our sense of ourselves. We are people who value human rights. Third, we are signatories of international documents that obligate us to further human rights.

Q Haven't there been instances where our emphasis on human rights proved detrimental to our national interest?

A I know of none.

Q How do you answer arguments that our stand en-

[4] Reprint of interview with Patricia M. Derian, former Assistant Secretary of State for Human Rights. *U.S. News & World Report.* 90:49–50. Mr. 2, '81.

couraged the overthrow of pro-U.S. governments in Iran and Nicaragua?

A In both instances we put those dictatorial, tyrannical leaders—the Shah and Somoza—into power and kept them there for 30 years with our support. Finally, the people who had to live under the tyranny of each of these despots reached the point of revolution. It was not the human-rights policy of our government that brought about the revolutions.

Q Some critics say that human rights are an internal matter for each country and therefore none of our business—

A I can't believe that in 1981 anyone would advance such an argument. Internal matters affect the world community. Was it none of our business when Hitler decimated the Jews? When Stalin, who killed millions inside the Soviet Union, was, in the name of *Realpolitik*, effectively given Eastern Europe? And when today many people who want to leave the Soviet Union are still prevented from doing so? Or when millions were killed in mainland China? Curiously, I find people applying this argument of "none of our business" only to right-wing dictatorships—not to the Soviet Union.

In addition, a roomful of documents makes human rights a matter of international law and concern: The Helsinki Final Act of 1975, the Inter-American Declaration of the Rights and Duties of Man, the United Nations Universal Declaration of Human Rights.

Q How should the U.S. protect human rights in the world?

A There is a whole arsenal of tactics to be used. One is quiet diplomacy. You are sitting across a table from representatives of another government to discuss an official agenda, one item of which is human rights. Then there is the way you vote in the United Nations and what you say in lobbying for support of the U.S. position. There's also what you do in the Inter-American Human Rights Commission, in the U.N.'s Human Rights Commission and in the casting of U.S. votes in the international banks.

Q When would you withhold economic and military aid?

A U.S. law says that gross violators of human rights are not eligible for U.S. economic and military aid unless the President determines that a cutoff would be detrimental to U.S. national security or the aid goes to assist the poorest of the poor.

A good example of such a national-security exception is South Korea. As bad as its government's human-rights policies are, we certainly don't want the North Koreans to come in and take over. It would jeopardize regional security and our own, since we have a stake in the Pacific.

Q *Just how successful was the Carter administration in reducing repression around the world?*

A Very successful. Countless numbers of people are alive today because of our policy. Torture has been reduced somewhat. A number of countries have returned to civilian government. Thousands and thousands of people who were in prison are now free.

Indonesia is one example. In 1977, there were 30,000 people in jail who had been there for about 13 years—never charged, never tried, never sentenced; just stashed away. And now they're out. In Argentina, thousands of people had disappeared. Many of their bodies were found in the streets. Now, summary execution has practically stopped, though there is still torture, and disappearances do continue, but at a lower rate. In South Korea, opposition leader Kim Dae Jung is alive today largely because of the U.S. emphasis on human rights. There is almost no country where we cannot see some favorable consequences for individuals.

Q *What other effects did the policy have?*

A It strengthened human rights in a global way. The Inter-American Human Rights Commission is much stronger—largely due to the support of the United States. The U.N.'s Human Rights Commission, which for more than 10 years had done virtually nothing, has become an effective mechanism. The Organization of African Unity is now working diligently to establish a regional human-rights organization.

Also, as a result of the Carter policy you cannot now find a leader of any country who does not place hand on heart and swear fidelity to human rights. Such words are an important first step, even if actual progress is slow.

Q In what way did the Carter policy help the U.S. national interest?

A It greatly improved our image abroad. In 1977, citizens of many other countries tended to view our policies as completely self-centered. Now, as a result of four years of the Carter policy, much of that bad feeling about the U.S. has been washed away. This shows up clearly in international polls and in the attitude of foreign diplomats toward us.

Q What will happen to the human-rights policy under the Reagan administration?

A I can't predict. I keep hearing administration people say, "Well, we're going to practice quiet diplomacy," as though they were inventing the electric light for the first time. Until recently, human rights has not been a partisan political issue. It has had Republican as well as Democratic supporters. To turn it into a political football is to do a disservice to the country.

Copyright 1981, U.S. News & World Report, Inc.

TERRORISM VS. HUMAN RIGHTS[5]

If a government official were to announce that increased subsidies to agriculture would now "take the place" of food stamps, someone would be sure to ask what the two things had to do with one another and why it wouldn't be possible to have both. But when Secretary of State Alexander Haig told reporters at his first press conference since he assumed office that "international terrorism will take the place of human rights in our concern, because it is the ultimate abuse of human rights," no one thought to ask why the government had to choose between them. Nor did anyone ask how, if international terrorism really was the worst of the human-rights abuses, you could speak of one taking the place of the other. A hint of what the new policy was going to mean in action came during the recent visit to Washington of President

[5] Reprint of magazine article entitled "Notes and Comment." *New Yorker.* 56:31–2. F. 16, '81. Reprinted by permission; © 1981 The New Yorker Magazine, Inc.

Chun Doo Hwan, of South Korea, the general who seized power a few weeks after his predecessor, President Park Chung Hee, was assassinated. President Carter had held up important negotiations with South Korea on economic and military matters because of human-rights abuses there, but the Reagan Administration resumed the negotiations, and the State Department announced that hereafter the United States would not "go into the internal state of affairs in the Republic of Korea;" at the same time, the Department asked Congress to postpone publication of a report on human rights which was said to contain information that would embarrass President Chun. The impression one gained was that the United States was lowering its concern about human rights not in order to fight terrorism better but in order to more firmly cement its ties with repressive right-wing regimes around the world. President Reagan did not do anything to clarify Administration policy when, in an appearance with President Chun at a White House luncheon, he remarked that Korean and American soldiers had fought together in Korea and again in Vietnam, where "the cause was freedom," leaving one to wonder how there could be a crusade that was for freedom without also being for human rights. Since South Vietnam in the days of the Vietnam War enjoyed no more freedom than South Korea does now, one has to assume that the freedom President Reagan had in mind was our own—a freedom we really do possess but are willing to defend, it seems, by supporting regimes that deny freedom to their own people. (In his inaugural address, President Reagan, who has taken to claiming that God has a "divine plan" for the United States, said, "God intended for us to be free." He did not add that God intended South Korea or Vietnam to be free.) This policy is no novelty of the Reagan Administration—it has spanned many Administrations, and was only slightly disturbed by the Carter human-rights policy—and its cost to the United States has always been high. When the Soviet Union, a left-wing totalitarian nation, supports another left-wing totalitarian nation somewhere in the world, its action is consistent with its domestic policies and its beliefs. But when the United

States, a constitutional democracy, supports a right-wing dictatorship, our belief in freedom, or human rights, or liberty, or whatever you choose to call it—our reason for existing as a nation, and our mission, if we have one, in the world—goes unsupported and unspoken for in international affairs. Even though we may extend a network of arms all around the globe, freedom shrinks to a purely domestic matter—a sort of luxury, like our large gross national product, and one that is defended, but not enjoyed, by other peoples. Our foreign policy then becomes nothing more than a military shield, containing no reflection of the spirit of our country. One unfortunate consequence of this abdication of our beliefs on the international scene is that American protests against repression by the Soviets of their own people and others lose their force. (It seems notable that Mr. Haig chose "international terrorism" as his target and did not even mention Soviet violations of human rights.) But the greatest danger for the United States—one that came menacingly to life in the period of Vietnam and Watergate—is that we will eventually regard our political system, with its inefficient constitutional restraints and its inconvenient individual liberties, as an unnecessary obstacle in our grandiose global struggle for "freedom" (but not "human rights"). There are already a few signs that our love of liberty is being construed as weakness toward our enemies. In a recent editorial, the *Wall Street Journal* remarked that "in the Carter Administration 'human rights' were code words for a lurch toward accommodation of the international left." The international left itself, of course, including, especially, the Soviet Union, regarded Carter's human-rights program as a disguise for an anti-Soviet lurch toward the right. (The Soviets were especially angry when Carter sent Andrei Sakharov a letter of support.) Between these views, the actual substance of human rights gets interpreted out of existence. It is perhaps unsurprising that the Soviet Union and its friends should look upon American devotion to human rights as a cover for something else, but that we, too, should do so is a needless disfavor to ourselves.

HUMAN RIGHTS[6]

Air Date: February 10, 1981

ROBERT MacNEIL: ... The former Carter administration had its final say, so to speak, in foreign policy last night with the release of the annual report on human rights around the world. In addition to detailing how other governments treat their people, the report notes that the Congress directed that concern for human rights should be a principal goal of U.S. foreign policy. The Carter administration, of course, made it a very prominent and public goal. But the Reagan administration has made clear that it will give concern for human rights a lower profile. Secretary of State Haig told his first press conference that international terrorism will take the place of human rights as the priority concern of U.S. foreign policy. Secretary Haig returned to that theme last night in a speech here in New York, [when] he called rampant international terrorism "a heinous disease jeopardizing the fundamental freedom from fear." At that same dinner, CBS News correspondent Walter Cronkite said the U.S. future was tied to human rights and social justice, adding, "we are not made stronger by friends who are hated by the mass of their own people." That was a taste of what is shaping up as a growing debate about the Reagan emphasis on terrorism over human rights. Tonight, what did the Carter human rights campaign achieve, and is Mr. Reagan right to scrap it? Jim?

JIM LEHRER: Robin, the new report surveys 153 governments on human rights—all U.N. member countries are included, plus those which receive U.S. economic and military aid, and others of special interest to the United States. El Salvador, where 9000 people have died in the last year, received

[6] Transcript of interviews of Rita Hauser, former Representative to the UN Human Rights Commission; Patricia Derian, former Assistant Secretary of State for Human Rights; Walter Laqueur, historian; and Representative Don Bonker (D), Washington. *The MacNeil/ Lehrer Report*—Human Rights. F. 10, '81. Copyright © 1981 by Educational Broadcasting Corporation and GWETA. Reprinted by permission.

a lot of attention; so did the Soviet Union, Vietnam, and Bolivia, as well as South Korea and many others. It's a report
that is required by law. Every year the State Department
must submit it to the two main foreign affairs committees in
Congress. This one was more than 1000 pages long, com-
pleted and delivered four days before the inauguration. But it
was held until after the visit of South Korean President Chun,
in order to save embarrassment of what the report said about
his country. The report was compiled under the supervision
of the Carter administration's Assistant Secretary of State for
Human Rights, Patricia Derian. Ms. Derian was clearly the
point person for the Carter human rights policy. Most of
those who didn't like the policy included Ms. Derian promi-
nently in their criticisms. First, were you upset over the decision to hold up your report while South Korean President
Chun was here?

PATRICIA DERIAN: First of all, it was not my report. It was
the report of the United States Department of State. I wasn't
upset about it because it was actually a trifle. We are in the
midst of a real debate and discussion on the future of the policy. So whether the report comes out five days later, or five
days sooner, is really of no consequence to me. The only side
effect I see is that everybody who is interested in the report is
surely going to read the one on South Korea, so I'm not sure
that they actually achieved anything.

LEHRER: Well look, let me ask you this. In general terms, is
the state of the world on the question of human rights better
now than it was four years ago when the Carter administration launched its emphasis on human rights?

Ms. DERIAN: I don't know. I think you can point to some improvements; you can point to some regression; you can point
to some continuing severe problems. The point of the policy
is not so much a measurement; the point of the policy is essentially twofold: one, we underwrite through insurance,
through favorable loans, through assistance in selling—an
enormous number of American businesses who do business
abroad with other governments. In other words, we put the
seal of approval on the expenditure of American dollars and

the support for various kinds of arrangements between two countries. What we believe, and what the purpose of the law is, is that the United States should not give official sanction to repression of human beings by other governments through the use of the Export-Import Bank, through the use of our aid, through the use of our military equipment or military training. And so part of it is to just distance ourselves. We're the land of the free and the home of the brave; we've got no business propping up dictators with our money. That's the purpose of the policy, and the ancillary purpose, of course, is that you do what you can to improve the condition of human rights around the world.

LEHRER: There have been many criticisms, as you know, of the policy; foremost among them, that you operated under a double standard. You were hard on our little right-wing friends, and soft on our big left-wing enemies. How do you respond to that?

Ms. DERIAN: Utter nonsense. In the first place, we don't give aid or military assistance to the Soviet Union, for instance. But I think anybody who reads the report will get the flavor of the way that those countries were viewed. It's just arrant nonsense—there's almost no way to treat it seriously. Did we talk about the countries? Yes. We talked about all of them. Look at the congressional testimony. Look at the noon briefings. Go through my series of speeches.

LEHRER: Another criticism was that the whole approach was wrong; in other words, the public approach. They accused you and your colleagues—the President included—of engaging in moralistic rhetoric publicly when the best way, if you really wanted to clean up these countries, would have been to have done it through quiet diplomacy.

Ms. DERIAN: Well, quiet diplomacy is actually something that was used in the last four years. It was talked about much before 1977. Mostly what that meant was that some high official of this government would say to a high official of another government, "look, the Congress is driving us crazy. They don't understand your problems. Would you please let 'x' out of jail? Would you please change 'y' or 'z'?" What we did in the quiet diplomacy area was put it on the official agenda so that we sat across the table and discussed these matters in the same way that other bilateral problems were discussed between countries. And we did do that. We also responded to congressional initiative; that is, we obeyed the law, we printed these reports, and what is this—that we should be quiet when people are torturing others? What is that? This is the United States of America. For God's sake! I can't imagine why we somehow have to pretend that people who are engaging in these practices of repression to hold onto power are somehow people we should be applauding. We did that with the Shah. It hasn't paid off for us, and certainly it didn't pay off in human rights terms.

LEHRER: Finally, and in a word, Ms. Derian, when you left office after four years—two-and-a-half or so weeks ago—did you leave with a sense that you had accomplished something in terms of human rights around the world?

Ms. DERIAN: Oh, yes. There's so much to be done, it is a task forever. But I think that the view of this country has changed markedly. That is, that we are now perceived once again as a principled people who try very hard to behave in the way that they say their beliefs go. . . .

MacNEIL: Now to someone who approves of the Reagan change of emphasis. She is Rita Houser, an international lawyer who served as the U.S. representative on the United Nations human rights commission from 1969 to 1973. Most recently, Ms. Hauser served as a member of the Reagan foreign policy advisory group. Ms. Hauser, did the Carter human rights policy work, in your view?

RITA HAUSER: In some instances it did; in some instances it didn't. What I would take the sharpest criticism with is the fact that it became an end all in itself rather than part of an overall approach to any one given country that one must always engage in—a pragmatic approach. You cannot simply isolate human rights from considerations that are military, diplomatic, economic, strategic. In some instances, we can work with strong tools; in others we have to go with *sotto voce;* in others we have to use the quiet diplomacy. In other instances, the open diplomacy will suffice. There is no one remedy that applies across the board.

MacNEIL: Can you be pragmatic without being cynical, and without turning a blind eye to human rights violations in places where it may be convenient to do that—some friendly country?

Ms. HAUSER: Again, they are firstly questions of degree. When a country passes beyond a certain heinous point of degree—Nazi Germany—beyond that there is no, in my view, no discussion of any other considerations. It has become a murderous regime in toto. I don't think we face—thank goodness—too many of those situations, although there are a few operative now in Asia. Other countries will fall more in a grey area. Let's take an illustration of Argentina, a friendly country, a country with which we have a good bit of leverage, where some of the Carter diplomacy did succeed, and where in certain instances, it didn't succeed. And I think that is probably the best test case to look at. Or Iran, where we will debate for a very long time whether what we did had a role in the fall of the Shah. I personally believe that it is impossible to look at human rights except in pragmatic terms. Some countries we're going to have to deal with and play down the human rights issue even though we don't like it, because there are other integral considerations that we must look at. South Africa, a case in point. We can't afford to lose it. We can't afford to have it fall in the Soviet orbit; it is a very important country for us. We can't simply approach South Africa just on the basis of apartheid, and pretend that nothing else exists in the spectrum.

MacNEIL: Did the Carter administration do that?

Ms. HAUSER: I think so. I think its South African policy was very largely a failure, and led to a whole series of articles and suggestions by its supporters that we embargo its products, and we isolate it in the world community—instead of an approach that I would have fashioned, which would have been to offer it a carrot of coming into the defense system of the West provided it ameliorated an unacceptable policy.

MacNEIL: Well, now, turning to the Reagan administration, can we use South Africa as an example? How is it likely to change under the Reagan administration as you understand the policy?

Ms. HAUSER: I don't think the policy has been fashioned yet, so I'm speaking of my own guesswork as to it, but I would think that the importance—the enormous strategic and military importance, and economic importance of South Africa—would weigh heavily in the thinking. We would sit down with the South African leadership and say. "You want to be part of the western alliance? You've got to make certain concessions now, major changes on the policy of apartheid, which is unacceptable to the rest of the western world." And use it as an effective carrot to bring them in rather than to denounce them, to call for their ostracism in the United Nations, or otherwise to make them into a pariah nation. Which was where the Carter policy was veering toward.

MacNEIL: That would actually be a tougher policy in a sense.

Ms. HAUSER: In many ways, but a more pragmatic one. My criticism of the Carter policy was that it wasn't significantly pragmatic and realistic.

MacNEIL: Ms. Derian's probable [successor], Dr. Ernest Lefever, is a man who criticized the Carter policy very roundly, and is reputed to have—I haven't read his writings—but is reputed to have a very scornful attitude to that kind of concern for human rights. You do know him. How do you think—assuming his appointment goes through—he would conduct it? [Lefever's name was later withdrawn—Ed.]

Ms. HAUSER: Well, I think Ernie's views have been distorted. He's a man of deep commitment to human rights, and has been for a very long time—in as many years as I have known him. I think he would take an approach similar to the one that I have just outlined to you which is a nuanced program. Obviously, the United States is not, under Reagan or anybody else, winding up supporting intolerable regimes for no other reason than it doesn't work. As Walter Cronkite effectively said—I think he summed it up well enough—if the regime is repressive enough, there will be a violent upheaval at some point against it, and we would be left very much on the short end of that politically.

MacNEIL: Well, thank you. We hear now from a man who has dealt with the issues of terrorism and human rights for years. He is historian Walter Laqueur, chairman of the Research Council of the Georgetown Center for Strategic and International Studies. He's the coauthor of a collection of writings called *The Human Rights Reader.* His most recent book is *The Terrible Secret,* the story of the Nazi assault on human rights. Dr. Laqueur, do you agree with de-emphasizing human rights to mount a campaign against terrorism?

Dr. WALTER LAQUEUR: No, I don't agree. I think it's wrong by itself, and it's wrong as far as effectiveness of American foreign policy is concerned.

MacNEIL: You don't think it should be de-emphasized?

Dr. LAQUEUR: I don't think it should. I think it's—I hope it's a temporary aberration; it's a reaction, probably an overreaction against certain things which happened in recent years.

MacNEIL: Do you believe that the concern should be continued as an instrument of American foreign policy as publicly and as outspokenly as it has been?

Dr. LAQUEUR: Yes. I think so. I think that emphasizing secret diplomacy, and private talk—well, sometimes it does help, but usually it doesn't.

MacNEIL: Secretary Haig said at his first press conference that international terrorism is, to use his words, is the greatest problem in the area of human rights today. Do you agree with that?

Dr. LAQUEUR: Well, I hold no brief for international terrorism, but—and indeed it's a threat because terrorists have no great respect for human rights. But I would imagine it's more a problem for police, or say, the CIA, and I do not really think it's the world's most foremost problem now. There's not more terrorism going on now than a few years ago, and we're all against it. We think action is needed. But I don't quite see the direct connection here with human rights.

MacNEIL: What is international terrorism, in your definition?

Dr. LAQUEUR: Here again, in a way, I'm a purist. I'm sure when Secretary of State Haig came out against international terrorism, he didn't mean he's in favor of national terrorism; however, we all know that there are certain connections. We know that the Soviet Union has a certain interest in destabilizing certain countries—Turkey, for instance—and [I] could mention others, and publicity should be given; measures should be taken against it. Broadly speaking, terrorism—or international terrorism—is the attempt of a minority to impose by violent means its wish on the majority.

MacNEIL: Would you include repression of people by their own government as acts of terrorism?

Dr. LAQUEUR: Well, there's a great deal of evil in the world, but not every act is terrorism. No, of course there's state terrorism, but at the moment we include these kind of things, there is no limit. Then everyone is a terrorist and no one is a terrorist. It's dangerous.

MacNEIL: In your view, is this new policy of emphasizing terrorism as Secretary Haig again did in his speech last night, another way of saying—a kind of code way of saying —let's get tougher with the Soviet Union and international communism?

Dr. LAQUEUR: Yes and no, because I don't really think the Soviet Union is the only offender and the only opponent. Most of these things are very carefully laundered. Other countries come in. And it's a complicated matter . . .

LEHRER: Finally the views of a congressman who has supported the Carter human rights policy. He's Congressman Don Bonker, Democrat of Washington State, chairman of the House Subcommittee on Human Rights and International Organizations. Congressman, are you prepared to replace human rights with international terrorism as a foreign policy priority for this country?

Rep. DON BONKER: Well, I really don't see the incompatibility between the two. Indeed, terrorism is a form of human rights violation, and it doesn't matter whether it takes place aboard a hijacked plane, or whether it's the Red Brigade in Italy, or whether victims of a repressive regime in Latin America. It's a form of violation of human rights, and that's how it ought to be considered.

LEHRER: So you don't think there's going to be any problem, then, in terms of a priority change; it's all part of the same— it's all part of the same package.

Rep. BONKER: Oh, I think it is. That's why I doubt there is a distinction that the new Secretary was attempting to make.

LEHRER: You mean you think it was a rhetoric change rather than a reality change?

Rep. BONKER: Well, rhetoric or emphasis. Nobody's for international terrorism. By stressing that issue, you carry a popular appeal with the people, but in substance it doesn't mean very much.

LEHRER: As I said in introducing you, you basically supported the Carter administration's human rights policy. How would you judge it in terms of what it accomplished?

Rep. BONKER: Well, I think it accomplished a great deal both in terms of a global consciousness that both the oppressed and the oppressor are now far more sensitive to human rights conditions. I don't think rulers nowadays can ignore the international awareness about human rights in their own countries. But also in various ways, and through Pat Derian's efforts, we were able to influence government policies in various countries that have resulted in lives being saved, and in the lowering of repression that has been so prominent in the past few decades.

LEHRER: What do you think of Ms. Hauser's nuanced approach—to use her term. What's your reaction to the policies she laid out as a substitute in a way for what the Carter people did?

Rep. BONKER: Well, I think first of all, we shouldn't make the distinction between the Carter administration and the Reagan administration. It's premature because we don't have any real comparison to make. But it should be pointed out that almost all of the human rights policies that we know about today are of Congress, not necessarily of the Carter administration. Since 1974, there has been a consistent pattern of amendments to the Foreign Assistance Act both in terms of cutting off aid to countries who engage in a consistent pattern of human rights violations, in terms of statutes which instruct our representative to the international financial lending community to vote against various loans and technical assistance to these countries, and in various other ways, Congress has spoken, and spoken with a bipartisan voice, equally applying our human rights policies to authoritarian regimes on the right, and leftist regimes in communist countries.

LEHRER: Do you believe that it's going to continue to speak with one voice?

Rep. BONKER: Oh I think so, and if the new administration feels that they can abandon our human rights policies, they're going to have to do that in a way that violates our statutes which are firmly in place, and supported in a bipartisan manner in both the Senate and the House of Representatives.

LEHRER: Of course, the administration has not said they're going to abandon the policy, all they say is that they're going to change priorities, but that doesn't bother you at all, does it?

Rep. BONKER: Well, I'm concerned that our law is followed in terms of submission of this report which gives a country-by-country account, and in various other ways that we have acted in the Congress. Now, it could be that the Reagan administration will do to the human rights policy what the Nixon administration did to ACTION and poverty programs. That is, keep them in place but really de-emphasize them to a point where they've rendered the program meaningless.

LEHRER: Is the program rendered meaningless if it is not as public as the Carter implementation was? In other words, there has to be a Pat Derian issuing reports and criticizing the governments for the policy to work?

Rep. BONKER: Well, I think that it's all open and on public record now. Not only is the State Department report distributed widely, but Amnesty International has a report. There are over 40 human rights organizations in Washington D.C. alone. So I don't think any country now can escape its responsibilities to its own citizens. What our country does, with respect to those violations is the question, and I can't imagine that people are going to allow their tax dollars to be used to support regimes on the right or on the left that deny their own people basic human rights . . .

MacNEIL: Ms. Derian, to put this very simply, are you concerned that under the new policy, some people might actually die or be tortured or remain in prison who might have been spared had the Carter policy remained in force?

Ms. DERIAN: I'll tell you, I was just sitting here wishing that Rita Hauser were going to take my old job. Because what she described is exactly what we have been doing for the last four years, and it's intriguing to me—I don't know whether it's because people who are on the other side politically saw this—and I don't mean Ms. Hauser at this point—but during the campaign, whether someone chose this as a partisan political issue. The fact of it is that the human rights policy has never been partisan. It is not conducted in a partisan way, it doesn't go against right or against left; it just simply marches along using international standards and our own view of ourselves as a people. So I'm not going to make a neat headline tonight and say that I think it would be death-bringing for the Reagan people to proceed the way that we think that they're going to go—if anybody would ever say how they're going to go beyond that odd statement of Secretary Haig's about international terrorism. So what I hope is that they're going to get in there, find out what it is we have been doing, find out what the law is, find out what needs to be done, and get on with it.

MacNEIL: Ms. Hauser, could you be sure in your own mind when you go to bed at night that under the new administration nobody in another country was going to die—to put it very crudely—who might otherwise have been spared because of U.S. pressure?

Ms. HAUSER: Well, that's crude because I don't know that U.S. pressure per se ever produces any one particular result. That's not the way to look at it. I will go to bed comfortable with the knowledge that President Reagan is as committed to the saving of human life, and the avoidance of deprivation of human rights as any of his predecessors or his successors. That isn't what we're talking about. We're talking about modalities—ways of operating, the best methods of achieving results. Failure to bring the policy to a highly moralistic level, which is what President Carter tended to do over and over in judgmental values. You don't need judgmental values too often in international politics. You need to find pragmatic solutions: how can we best effectuate a change that we'd like to do consistent with all our other relations, and all our other interests? It isn't easy.

Ms. DERIAN: But you do have principles—

Ms. HAUSER: Of course you have principles.

Ms. DERIAN: —that you stand by, and I'm not sure it's so moralistic to live by your own principles. That's the pragmatic approach. So that other countries know who you are and know what to expect and what your principles are: that you stand for things squarely. Of course you must operate pragmatically, but you must also operate in a principled way, and I think that that's falling into a decision about whether it's going to be principled or whether it's going to be pragmatic as though there were some cleavage there, when there's no reason for there to be one at all.

MacNEIL: Is there no room for cleavage there?

Ms. HAUSER: Well, I think it's very clear that the United States operate principally as a given. I suppose there have been exceptions from time to time, but we operate on a basis of our established principles, and we try to foster all of the goals that are part of our inherent foreign policy. But one can't wind up, for example, alienating a very important country to us because we take an approach on human rights which is nonreceptive. You have to find another way of doing it. Argentina, I think, was another case in point where some of the policy worked, but some of it certainly served to alienate that government from us . . .

LEHRER: Dr. Laqueur, what's your view of that? Can you have a human rights policy that is both moralistic and pragmatic, or do the two cancel each other out?

Dr. LAQUEUR: They do not necessarily cancel each other

out. But, you see, the present administration, of course, reacts
and, as I said maybe overreacts, because of their weaknesses
during the last four years. One starts with a wonderful concept and I'm sure Pat Derian started with, and has best intentions, but then in the real world one has to make concessions. One country one should be careful because it has
nuclear weapons, and another country has oil, and the third
country—I believe, to give you an example, this report which
came out yesterday—there is no section about Iran. Why is
there no section about Iran? Because of the hostages. I don't
think if there would have been a section on Iran, the hostages
would not have been released. So the point I try to make is
[that] to be effective, there has to be consistency. Of course,
again, there have to be concessions, but there has to be limits
to concessions. I think there were too many concessions.

LEHRER: Congressman, what's your view of the pragmatic
approach as outlined by Ms. Hauser?

Rep. BONKER: Well, I don't believe the two are incompatible. I think we have a moral base upon which we make certain foreign policy decisions, and there has to be a certain
pragmatism that goes into those decisions. I recall a while
back when Assistant Secretary of State Christopher appeared
before our committee, and he headed up the so-called task
force that would review our assistance to various countries,
and their compliance with human rights standards. And he
listed four countries that would receive reduced aid because
of their human rights problems. One of those countries was
Pakistan. And that was before Russia invaded Afghanistan.
Shortly thereafter that happened. And we then quickly provided $500 million in military assistance to Pakistan. All of a
sudden, our human rights concern was not explicit in our foreign policy.

LEHRER: Does that bother you? Or is that legitimate?

Rep. BONKER: Well, it bothered me at the time, but it hints
at the pragmatism. We have to have human rights as a factor
among many that has to go into foreign policy decision-mak-
ing.

THE COMMON SENSE OF HUMAN RIGHTS[7]

Recently, on NBC network news, we were informed that the United States was contemplating sending arms to Pakistan, as part of a new military alliance. Immediately following the transmission of this bit of "hard news," we were further informed that Pakistan is a nation where the legal code still permits the public flogging of criminals and where the political opposition is repressed. In this way we were given notice by the media that an alliance with Pakistan creates a serious "human rights" problem for us.

Does it? To give a reasonable answer to that question would require thoughtful reflection on the whole issue of human rights, something that has not been a notable characteristic of current controversy. Instead, we have been treated mainly to vacuous moralism, hypocritical and tendentious exposes, and (more recently) a "hard-headed realism" that tends to evade the issue altogether. If we are ever to integrate an idea of human rights into our foreign policy, as I think we must, we are not going about it very successfully.

I want to emphasize that we really must integrate a conception of human rights into our foreign policy—into our alliances, our military aid programs, our economic aid programs, our cultural exchanges, etc: Our polity, after all, is founded on the idea of an individual's rights. Our foreign policy, to the degree that it rubs this idea the wrong way, will be guilt-ridden, uncertain, lacking in self-confidence. The United States never has had, never can have, and in my view never should try to have a purely "geopolitical" foreign policy. Elements of *Realpolitik* will surely have to be incorporated into our foreign policy, as in all foreign policies. But such "realism" has

[7] Reprint of article by Irving Kristol, Professor of Social Thought at the NYU Graduate School of Business, a Senior Fellow of the American Enterprise Institute and a member of the *Journal's* board of contributors. *Wall Street Journal.* 197:28. Ap. 8, '81. © 1981 by the *Wall Street Journal.*

to be conceived and expressed in a way that allows us to live, if a bit uncomfortably now and then, with our moral selves.

Integration Principles

So how do we go about achieving the desirable and necessary integration? Are there principles governing any such integration? I think there are. Moreover, I do not think they are particularly esoteric principles discernible only to the sophisticated political philosopher. Rather, I believe they are already fully, if implicitly, possessed by American popular opinion, are in accord with the "common sense" upon which such opinion rests, but are badly in need of articulation.

Let us see if we can elucidate the principles that are needed successfully to incorporate the idea of human rights into American foreign policy. There are, I would say, five such principles.

(1) The American idea of human rights involves rights *against government.* It is important to emphasize this because postwar liberalism has purposefully expanded the idea of human rights to include a whole spectrum of "entitlements," identified as "rights," that are to be satisfied *by* government. The various United Nations declarations and resolutions, which list as "human rights" such items as vacations with pay, maternity leave, full employment and free medical care, are illustrative of this tendency. The American government, in its moments of silliness, has actually signed such declarations and resolutions. But the American people never have subscribed to any such nonsense.

Actually, it is a rather dangerous piece of nonsense. Such a conception of "human rights" permits left-wing ideologues to claim that, while the United States has a better record than, say, the Soviet Union or Cuba in certain areas of human rights, these latter nations can claim superiority in other areas—so, in sum, there really is no absolute difference, no difference in principle, between us and them. Indeed, the whole point of such a radical expansion of the idea of "human rights" is to minimize the importance of individual liberty as the keystone of that idea.

This permits dozens of nations to make solemn speeches in the UN in favor of "human rights" while blandly restricting and repressing individual liberty at home.

It would be a blessing if the United States began to move openly and deliberately to dissociate itself from this UN smokescreen. That would assuredly cause an enormous flap, both at the UN and among our own liberal folk. But it would be well worth while.

(2) Rights against government are to be distinguished from democratic rights—i.e., rights to participate *in* self-government. Though it is natural for Americans to wish to see all peoples govern themselves more or less as we do, it is obvious that the world is full of peoples who, as things now stand, are unable or unwilling to do so. The United States does have a missionary vocation for democracy—but only to the extent that our successful example encourages others to emulate us.

It is not really for us to insist that any or every country should have free elections or universal suffrage—that is their affair. We do, however, have a historic mission to defend the rights of the individual against arbitrary or tyrannical government, whether that government expresses the popular will or (as is more often the case) does not. It is a mission that has been an organic aspect of our very self-definition as a nation, ever since its origins.

(3) In reality, of course, there are always more complications, more shades and varieties of repression, than abstractions about human rights can cope with. So it is useful to have a workable set of priorities in mind. It seems to me that there are four human rights which are of such prime significance to Americans that, when any nation violates them, we promptly have a problem in our relations with that nation. They are:

☐ The practice of torture—not "harsh treatment" but literal torture—against political opponents is so fundamentally obnoxious as to be always and everywhere unacceptable to us. Torture is an assault on the metaphysical concept of human dignity itself, from which our belief in individual rights is derived. Where its presence has been demonstrated, we ought to make our disapproval clear in every possible way.

☐ The right to emigrate is the most basic of all individual rights, since it tends automatically to set limits to what an authoritarian or totalitarian regime can do. (The relative "liberalism" of Communist Yugoslavia is certainly connected with the freedom of emigration it permits.) I regard it as nothing less than a scandal that our representatives to the UN have, over the years, deliberately ignored this issue, presumably for fear of offending Soviet sensibilities.

☐ Religious toleration is an idea so fundamental to the American way of life, so rooted in American traditions, that we simply cannot be indifferent to violations of that idea. Mind you, I am talking about religious toleration—i.e., freedom from religious persecution—not religious equality, and definitely not separation of church and state. These last are American ideas, not necessarily exportable. If a nation wishes to have a state-established religion, with special privileges, that is its affair. But freedom from religious persecution is a human right whose universality we must insist on.

Here again, our official and utter indifference to the violation of this human right—an indifference so visible at the UN—is a major scandal. Why haven't those representatives at the UN criticized the current government of Iran for its vicious persecution of the Bahais? When was the last time those representatives denounced the Soviet Union for persecuting pious Christians, Jews and Moslems? One suspects that this reflects the secular temper of the State Department, the media, the intellectual community. But we can be certain it does not reflect the temper of the American people.

☐ The rights of racial minorities were not always thought by Americans to represent a fundamental human right, but they have unquestionably acquired that status in recent decades. A nation which fails to recognize those rights inhabits a different moral universe from us and is unacceptable as friend and ally. Again, as with religion, it is not a question of political rights but of civil rights. In America, we insist that racial and religious minorities are entitled to both classes of rights. But American practice may not be readily exportable to other multi-racial or multi-religious societies. In contrast, our idea of individual civil rights—involving access to due process of law and protection of an individual's property and personal security—is one which we indeed take to be universal.

(4) Recently, discussions of human rights have often hinged on the distinction between "totalitarian" and "authoritarian" countries. It is, I believe, a valid distinction and provides some rough guidelines for our human rights policies. Totalitarian states deny *in principle* our idea of human rights, and will tend habitually to violate all of them. Authoritarian regimes merely assert the irrelevance of our idea to their reality, and in both theory and practice will recognize at least some of the fundamental rights I have made reference to.

Hope for an Evolution

Under authoritarian regimes there is always some ground for hope for an evolution toward a more liberal system. (We have witnessed that very evolution in Spain.) Totalitarian regimes exist precisely to rule out the possibility of any such evolution. Our attitudes toward these two very different kinds of illiberal system are bound to reflect these realities.

(5) In the real world of international power politics we are always forced, more frequently than we would like, to compromise our principles. There is nothing immoral about the American government's bowing to this inevitability. What is wrong, however, is for the government not to explain candidly to its people exactly why it is doing so. This may ruffle the sensibilities of some foreign governments—but that is a price we should insist they be prepared to pay.

In extreme situations, of course, discussions of human rights become a luxury, and the governing principle then becomes: The enemy of our enemy is our friend. Just when a situation is so extreme it is not easy to say, short of actual armed conflict. There are not, thank goodness, many places in the world today where our foreign policy is entrapped in such dire extremity—which is why I believe that the isssue of human rights is a real one and has to be integrated, better than it has been, into a realistic foreign policy.

LEFT-WING AND RIGHT-WING VIOLATIONS[8]

Writing in the *Wall Street Journal* on May 29, Irving Kristol lashed out at "the different attitudes of our human rights activists toward Huber Matos and Jacobo Timerman." Timerman, of course, is the Argentine journalist who was imprisoned, tortured, and exiled by the Argentine military authorities. Matos, as Kristol notes, was one of the principal leaders of the Cuban revolution. When he tried to resign his post as military governor of the Camaguey province in October 1959, Castro had him arrested. Matos was accused of "slandering the revolution" and was sentenced to 20 years in prison after a kangaroo-court trial at which Castro delivered a seven-hour harangue from the witness box. Ironically, Matos's "slander" was confined to the suggestion that Cuba was being led down the road to communism. But Kristol doesn't dwell on the injustices that both Matos and Timerman suffered. He points instead to the discrepancy between the attention given the two cases, and suggests this supports his claim that the human rights movement is controlled by forces among "the left and liberal-left" with "sophisticated political intentions."

Kristol was right to emphasize the similarities between Matos's and Timerman's experiences. Both men supported the ascent to power of the regimes that eventually turned on them. Both were imprisoned and tortured for speaking out in defense of individual freedoms and democratic and legal processes. Refusing to renounce their principles in the face of in-

[8] Reprint of article entitled "Kristol Unclear," by John Lieber, Harvard undergraduate and intern on staff of *New Republic*. *New Republic*. 184:18–19. Je 27, '81. Copyright 1981 by The New Republic. Reprinted by permission.

timidation, both were singled out for particularly brutal treatment during their incarcerations.

But Kristol is not the only one to notice the parallel. In his May 10 review of Timerman's book, *Prisoner Without a Name, Cell Without a Number,* Anthony Lewis took pains to compare the treatment that Timerman and Matos received. Kristol undoubtedly counts Lewis, the most ardent promoter of Timerman's story, among those with "sophisticated political intentions." But whatever Kristol may think of Lewis's foreign policy views in general, the reference to Matos made the obvious and necessary point: it is impossible to overlook the similarity between the methods of political repression practiced by right-wing and left-wing tyrannies.

It is precisely this conclusion that Kristol, and the present administration, find so threatening. Hence the effort to demonstrate that the people promoting Timerman—opponents of the fashionable theory that distinguishes "authoritarian" from "totalitarian" regimes—are as soft on left-wing tyranny as Kristol is on its right-wing counterpart. Kristol writes:

Finally freed, Mr. Matos is now in the United States, where the self-styled 'human rights movement' studiously ignores him. The *New Yorker* has not published his memoirs, as it has Mr. Timerman's. He has not been shepherded to Washington to influence the Senate Foreign Relations Committee's attitude toward the nominee for assistant secretary of state for human rights—as Mr. Timerman was. Mr. Timerman is a hero of the human rights crusade, Mr. Matos is consigned to the shadows. Can anyone believe this is accidental?

Is Kristol complaining about the professional human rights organizations that have excluded or forgotten Matos? Or about the press? Or about liberal legislators? Kristol probably finds all of the above negligent in guarding against left-wing totalitarianism. But the "human rights movement" is only a loosely knit community, insufficiently organized to do anything "studiously."

Kristol would have us infer that there is a conspiracy of silence against Matos. His insinuation that Matos's writings have not been widely disseminated because editors at magazines like the *New Yorker* are indifferent to political persecution by left-wing governments is not merely foolish, it is misleading. Timerman has published a book which, as even Kristol admits, can only move one to "compassion and outrage." But contrary to what Kristol implies, Matos's memoirs haven't been ignored—they simply haven't been published yet. And by all accounts, there has in fact been great interest in Matos's forthcoming book (which he expects to finish by the end of this year). Publishers and periodicals have been clamoring for excerpts and the rights to the book.

Nor is there reason to suggest that the media ever purposefully ignored Matos while extolling Timerman. When Timerman and Matos were released in June and October 1979, they were accorded approximately equal coverage. Most major US newspapers ran profiles or interviews with Matos at the time of his release. Both the *New York Times* and the *Washington Post* published front-page articles recounting the story of Castro's betrayal and describing the treatment Matos endured throughout his confinement. Timerman received the same kind of attention, though on a smaller scale. One does not automatically conclude from this that the media was biased against Timerman, but rather that Matos's 20-year imprisonment was seen to warrant more coverage than Timerman's three-year term.

Since his release Matos has devoted himself to organizing the democratic opposition to Castro in the Cuban exile community. He has not become a full-time advocate of worldwide human rights causes, which is not to say that Matos shares Kristol's suspicion of the institutionalized human rights movement. Speaking last week at a Washington ceremony celebrating the 20th anniversary of Amnesty International, Matos empahsized his "great resepct" for that organization, whose efforts were central in obtaining his release. Matos was one of seven former "prisoners of conscience" who were honored and spoke that night. Four of those seven had suffered under governments that Kristol would identify as "totalitarian." So much for the claim that the human rights movement conveniently overlooks "the threat from the totalitarian left."

Kristol was especially perturbed by Timerman's silent

presence at Ernest Lefever's confirmation hearings. After all, Timerman's book has proved inconvenient for Lefever and has called into question many of the ideas to which both Kristol and Lefever subscribe. But would Matos, as Kristol implies, have been more sympathetic toward Lefever? It doesn't seem likely. In a November 1979 letter to President Carter, Matos credited the president's human rights policy with having helped to secure his release. He wrote that it "has been not only a great moral stimulus for Cuban political prisoners, but also an important support in facing abuses in Cuban jails." When interviewers have sought his opinion of the repressive right-wing regimes of Latin America, Matos always has maintained that he abhors all governments that abridge the liberty of their people through violence and intimidation. It's difficult to reconcile this kind of attitude with Kristol's preference for a selective human rights policy. Would Kristol be sympathetic to Huber Matos if he were fighting Batista's "benign" dictatorship in the Sierra Maestra today?

KIRKPATRICK'S FOUR DISTINCTIONS[9]

In a single speech, delivered in early March to the Council on Foreign Relations in New York, Jeane Kirkpatrick, U.S. Ambassador to the United Nations, shed more light on the subject of human rights and national policy than all the candlepower of the UN Human Rights Commission has shed in a generation. Her statement has liberating force. Such is said about those few statements which cause the scales to fall from one's eyes, even as it happened to Saint Paul. Mrs. Kirkpatrick talked about four distinctions "crucial" to a consideration of human rights and national policy. They are worth memorizing.

The first of these is the distinction "between ideas and institutions." If you will read the United Nations Declaration of

[9] Excerpted from article by William F. Buckley, Jr. *National Review.* 33:688–9. Je. 12, '81. Copyright 1981, National Review, Inc. Reprinted by permission.

Human Rights and the accompanying documents you will find a classic confusion of the two. The Declaration speaks about everything from the right to a fair trial, to the right to choose one's profession, to the right to self-government. Mrs. Kirkpatrick correctly insists that to *have*, let us say, democracy, is entirely different from envisioning it. A society in which the minority, defeated at the polls, declines to accept the political authority of the majority, mandated at the polls, cannot practice democracy. It can only dream about it. In such a society, the idea of democracy exists; but its institutionalization has yet to be. The heresy of supposing that ideas can become institutions merely by affirming them is correctly depicted by Michael Oakeshott as "rationalism"—"making politics as the crow flies."

The second distinction is between "rights and goals." The most recent session of the United Nations Human Rights Commission affirmed a "right to development." In order to have that right, all you have to do is take an undeveloped society, give it peace, order, an ethos, economic liberty, and capital. Such indeed are the goals, or should be, of all countries. But getting from here to there is a problem. "Such declarations of human rights," said Mrs. Kirkpatrick, "take on the character, as one critic said, of a letter to Santa Claus." With mischievous practical effect. "When the belief that one has a right to develop coincides with the facts of primitive psychology, of caste systems, social hierarchies, societies based on ascription, on dictatorships—and those are, of course, the characteristics of very many societies in the world that claim the right to development—then the tendency to blame someone is almost overwhelming." That someone is generally: The West; and particularly the United States.

The third distinction is between "intention and consequence." Mrs. Kirkpatrick gives as a concrete example, El Salvador. There, fighting side by side with the insurrectionists, are men and women whose intentions are in no significant respect different from those of President Reagan or Secretary Haig. But to intend something—in this case, such freedom and justice as Salvadoran institutions will sustain—is not to achieve it. Accordingly, responsible policy asks, *What is the likely consequence* of a policy, not merely, What are the intentions of its supporters. Experience establishes that, when Communists are in control of the dissident or insurrectionary movement, what will happen is worse than what had been happening.

And, finally, there is the distinction between "personal morality and political morality." To define virtue for an individual, one need look no further than to the Bible. But political morality requires any number of things, the privatization of which we would hardly encourage. Things like armaments, treaties, balances of power, propaganda, disinformation, war . . . All these, in proper context, are expressions of political morality—which, successfully arranged, promote the possibility for the exercise of private morality.

FIRM RESISTANCE ON HUMAN RIGHTS[10]

The Reagan Administration has lost little time in directing U.S. foreign policy away from what it sees as a misplaced emphasis on human rights. But the responsibility of the executive branch for human rights did not begin in 1977 when President Carter signed the International Covenants on Civil and Political Rights and on Economic and Social Rights. It began at least as far back as 1948, when the United States led the United Nations in approving the Universal Declaration of Human Rights. Since then, this nation has joined many others in agreements and organizations to promote and monitor human rights, including the U.N. Commission on Human Rights, the Helsinki Final Act and the Inter-American Commission on Human Rights.

Furthermore, concern about human rights has been written into national law by Congress, which in 1973 amended the Foreign Assistance Act of 1961 to include observance of human rights as a condition for the reception of foreign aid. Since 1976, Congress has required an annual report from the

[10] Reprint of editorial. *America.* 144:220–1. Mr. 21, '81. Copyright America Press, 1981. Reprinted by permission.

State Department on the record of a growing list of nations concerning human rights. President Reagan's criticism, however, of the performance of the Carter Administration on human rights was that its initiatives on human rights had been selective and had proven ineffective.

Thus far, at least, the Reagan Administration has made little pretense of an even-handed approach to human rights. It has chosen, for instance, to overlook the international terrorism of the Letelier assassination, in which high-ranking officials of the Government of Chile were implicated. Instead the Administration invited Chile to join naval maneuvers this spring after lifting the ban on some economic aid to that nation. Again, the U.S. delegation to the U.N. Commission on Human Rights now sitting in Geneva appalled its friends by siding (along with the Soviet Union) with Argentina in its opposition to further investigations of those who have "disappeared" in that country. Within a day of a strong condemnation by the United Nations General Assembly of South Africa because it has reneged on its three-year-old agreement to settle the South West Africa question, President Reagan asked in a television interview, "Can we abandon a country that has stood beside us in every war we have fought?" Finally, the Argentine Government's new head, Lieut. Gen. Roberto Viola, was heading for a private visit with President Reagan and Secretary Haig on the day eight nonpolitical leaders of Argentina's human rights movement were arrested and their files on 6,000 "disappeared" persons seized.

The pattern seems to be emerging that "terrorism" is violence and repression practiced by nations aligned with the Communist bloc. Any violence and repression that happens to occur in nations friendly to the West is to be named something else rather more acceptable, like "security measures." To implement this struggle against terrorism, the Administration told the House Foreign Affairs and Senate Foreign Relations Committees on March 9, will require $7 billion in the security assistance budget and an extensive loosening of Congressional oversight of arms grants and sales.

Listening to that request was the chairman of the House

Subcommittee on Human Rights and International Organizations, Representative Don Bonker (D., Wash.), who had written recently in the Christian Science Monitor that "any attempt to dismantle or ignore our traditional commitment to human rights will be met with firm resistance in the Congress."

If he is right—and it is very important that he be right—the firm resistance should start immediately.

THE REAL CASE FOR HUMAN RIGHTS[11]

On Antisemitism

Human rights mean respect for human beings, recognition of each other's dignity. They mean cooperation, mutuality, negotiation. They mean the voice of reason. Yet imagine my shock when, in my very first days within this Commission, I heard, as I did hear in this room, so much hatred, so many lies, such squalid racism, such despicable antisemitism—all in the sacred name of human rights.

In 1945, there were only some fifty nations in the world, and these few established the United Nations. Today there are some 160 member nations; more than one hundred new states. Among these new nations stands tiny Israel. Israel is not a land rich in resources. It is a beautiful land. Yet much of it was for centuries desert land unsuitable for agriculture, and nearly bereft of significant industries.

Overcoming all obstacles, the Israelis have built a nation to rival any in the world in its sciences, its arts, its symphonies, its free press, its institutions of just and humane pro-

[11] Excerpted from four addresses by Michael Novak, chief United States delegate to the UN Commission on Human Rights. *National Review*. 33:364+. Ap. 3 '81. Copyright 1981, National Review, Inc. Reprinted by permission.

cedures. When some of my distinguished colleagues attempt
to portray Israel as a land without human rights, we must ask
them: Compared to what? Few nations have institutions, or
can exhibit to the public eye a record of humane practice, as
highly developed as those of Israel.

My new delegation—and new government—have learned
from history to honor the high spiritual achievement of Arab
culture, the brilliance, sensitivity, and natural courtesy of so
many of its citizens which we have experienced even in this
room. We respect its antiquity as a sophisticated and developed culture—an antiquity of which a new nation like ours
can only stand in awe. We admire the personal courage and
wisdom of many Arab leaders.

Our delegation is new, but the charges heaped against Israel before this Commission are old. They have long since
been aired, objectively examined, and discarded in the dust-
bin. The State of Israel is a fact. The Egyptian-Israeli peace
treaty is a fact. The Camp David accords are a fact. These are
realities to which passion must accommodate itself. They are
realities which ground future advances, future hopes.

The American people deeply admire a tone of reasoned
discourse, the demonstration of mutual respect, a dispassion-
ate sense of moderation and compromise—qualities which we
have often observed in the examples of Arab culture. But I am
afraid that the hatred, unreason, and wildness of language
manifested in this room—once they become more widely
known—are unlikely to be admired by the American people.
They have embarrassed, and often bored, this assembly.

On Terrorism

To understand the American concern with organized international terror, it is essential to understand the words of
James Madison, one of the architects of the American Constitution and its Bill of Rights. Human rights, Madison
forthrightly stated, are not established by writing words on
paper or by moving air with one's lips. Human rights are established by building specific types of institutions of quite

exact design. Human rights are established, further, when such institutions begin to live through organized, articulate, free, law-abiding interests—through free associations of every sort among a free people.

The enemies of human rights have finally grasped Madison's insight into how human rights actually are made real. They have grasped this insight not in order to realize it within their own societies, where it is absent, but to destroy it in other societies, where it has been embodied. They try to force defenders of existing human rights to abandon them in self-defense.

Where there is only terror, a Hobbesian state of nature exists—a war of all against all, murder from every side. In the years to come, my government will have more to say—and to do—on this subject. The resolution before us [on international terrorism] is like an arrow directed at an important target. Alas, the resolution falls short, and far off to one side, of the bull's-eye.

On Self-Determination

The agenda item we are now discussing has long been a priority of this commission. It has been called "the right of peoples to self-determination, and its application to peoples under colonial or alien domination or foreign occupation."

The words "foreign occupation" have only recently been added to the traditional phrasing. According to Lenin, socialism is never the cause of imperialism. Lenin should have lived to see this hour. For these words "foreign occupation" reflect sad developments in world affairs. It is no longer peoples subject to colonial domination who are deprived of their inalienable right to self-determination. Systems of "satellites" have been formed, invasions have been launched, and "foreign occupation" has become a new widespread reality over much of the world's surface.

Nowhere in the world has the principle of self-determination been more directly and flagrantly violated than in Afghanistan. Imagine the Afghans—a people that have imme-

morially resisted foreign occupation. Imagine their humilia-
tion. Imagine their suffering during this winter. Imagine their
resolve.

In December of 1979 the Soviet Union, giving way to
temptation in Afghanistan, sent massive flights of airplanes,
and long lines of trucks and tanks, outside the Soviet Union
and onto foreign soil. The Soviet Union clumsily pretended
that its troops had been invited by the government of Kabul.
Unfortunately, the head of the government which was alleged
to have requested Soviet assistance, Mr. Amin, was soon una-
vailable to testify to the accuracy of this claim. He was assassinated even as Soviet media were citing his request for Soviet
assistance. His successor, Mr. Babrak Karmal, has been understandably careful not to offend the Soviets. In this situation what we must do is evident. This Commission should
condemn the Soviet Union for its denial of self-determination
to the Afghan people.

I turn now to the tragic situation in Southeast Asia. The
brutal repression of human rights in Kampuchea has been before this Commission for several years. The case of Kampuchea now rightfully comes before us under a new agenda item
of self-determination. For the tragic abuses of the human
rights of the Kampuchean people continue—but now also
through a denial of their fundamental right of self-determination.

The Socialist Republic of Vietnam once defended the in-
humane role of the Pol Pot regime. Then it saw opportunity
and claimed to be the deliverer of the Kampucheans. It has
now replaced the Pol Pot regime as the persecutor of the
people of Kampuchea.

The Kampucheans remain under the iron hand of an army
of occupation ruling through a puppet regime. The Khmer
people have no voice in their political and economic system.
These abuses will not be corrected by the charade of an election run by the army of occupation, its results preordained.

The Vietnamese occupation continues in blatant violation
of the UN charter. It continues in defiance of resolutions
passed in the UN General Assembly by overwhelming ma-

jorities of the UN membership. It continues in contempt of the most recent demand by the foreign ministers of the non-aligned nations meeting in New Delhi. It continues in betrayal of all ideals of national liberation.

My delegation will support resolutions that call for withdrawal of forces of occupation from Afghanistan and from Kampuchea. We urge the new colonialist powers from which these forces originate to comply with these resolutions and with previous resolutions of the United Nations General Assembly and Security Council. We urge these nations to return to their often-stated ideals about national liberation.

On the Right to Development

Mr. Chairman, in addressing this item, my delegation finds it useful to translate the phrase "right to development" into terms rooted in our own experience. We are quite conscious of the fact that only two hundred years ago, our nation was a colony of a great European power. Our population numbered four million. Even one hundred years ago, we were a poor nation, full of promise, but quite undeveloped. In 1881, there were no airplanes, automobiles, electric lights, radios. The poverty of our frontier settlements and even of most of our cities was legendary. In 1881, no one spoke of a "right to development." But our nation had an opportunity to develop, perhaps even a responsibility to develop.

Development is an idea—an idea which entered the history of nations only in relatively recent times. When Julius Caesar first came to Geneva, he came by conveyances not much different from those used in every century afterwards until the early ninteenth century. Only then did the first steam railroad come into existence. Between Caesar's time and the year 1800, economic development occurred but only slowly. There was not much new under the sun.

Poverty and lack of development have been the main fact of human history. The first "inquiry into the nature and causes of the wealth of nations" did not occur until Adam Smith undertook it in 1776. Smith may properly be called the father of the idea of international economic development. Much, to be sure, has been learned since then. But his work was the decisive breakthrough. Wealth does have causes. Wealth can be created. The human race can learn how to escape from famine, misery, ignorance, and fear.

The fundamental purpose of democratic capitalism—the vision that sustains my nation and a score of others—is to reduce the material suffering of all mankind, to increase the wealth of all nations, so that all individuals may use their freedom as they choose.

In this Commission we have heard transnational corporations maligned. But no single institution has been so responsible for the great leap forward of economic development in this century as the private business corporation. The state is not the only instrument of development. Private individuals in voluntary association can also meet social challenges, pursue social goals, and heighten the common good. We have heard distinguished delegates in this room speak of "obscene profits." Are we to understand that losses are virtuous? Where there are no profits, there can be only losses or stagnation. But these are the exact opposite of development. Development itself is a form of profit—a reasonable return on investments made, a reasonable growth, a reasonable surge forward. On the whole, an economy without profit is an economy without development.

Our national road to development lay in trusting economic liberty first, in unleashing human energies from which bread—and more than bread—came. More often than not, totalitarians who take away political and civil rights in the name of bread produce less and less bread and—in addition—never do restore the rights they have usurped. In our close observation of the nations, we see that totalitarianism produces bread as poorly as it produces civil and political liberties.

No socialist nation on the Soviet model has yet experienced a revolution of political and civil rights in the direction of democracy. But other nations have. We believe that when citizens have economic liberties, inevitable pressures lead toward greater political and civil liberties. This is precisely why totalitarian regimes are stubbornly opposed to economic liberties. Their economies stagnate under strangling and suffocating bureaucracies, but they do not dare to bestow economic liberties—for in their train all other liberties follow.

WRONG ON HUMAN RIGHTS[12]

Jimmy Carter's human rights policy was far from perfect. It was oversold and sanctimonious, and the connection between American self-interest and human rights was never explained adequately. But these flaws do not justify the Reagan administration's wholesale derogation of the Carter policy or its adoption of a stance that seems to ignore human rights.

The Reagan case for reversing Carter policy is based on four premises which have gained wide acceptance, but which seriously misconstrue what the Carter policy was about. Here are the basic charges and the answers to them:

1) *The policy was a moral crusade incompatible with our real national security interests.* This argument fails to consider the potential damage to our national security from excessive support of repressive regimes. Although this support may gain short-run benefits, over the long run such regimes may get overthrown and our support may be resented by those who follow.

US human rights policy has separated us from official repression in countries like Brazil and South Africa. As a result, our interests are more likely to be protected if and when the current government falls. This *realpolitik* aspect of the human rights policy deserves more attention from critics and proponents alike.

2) *We were tough only on our non-communist friends and*

[12] Reprint of article by Stephen Cohen, former Deputy Assistant Secretary of State for Human Rights, now teaching at the Georgetown University Law Center. *New Republic.* 184:13–14. Mr. 28, '81. Copyright 1981 by The New Republic Inc. Reprinted by permission.

ignored our Soviet adversaries. Actually, Soviet human rights abuses were the subject of high-level attention from the earliest days of the Carter administration. It was President Carter who wrote to Andrei Sakharov and welcomed Alexander Solzhenitsyn to the White House (after President Ford had snubbed him) in order to publicize their harsh treatment by the Soviet government.

At conferences reviewing the Helsinki Accords, at Belgrade in 1978 and at Madrid in 1980, there was heavy pressure from our NATO allies to soft-pedal the human rights issue and avoid any mention of specific cases. But the Carter administration insisted on thorough and detailed review of Soviet violations.

3) *We applied a double standard, cutting off military aid only to non-communist countries.* The answer, of course, is that only non-communist countries are eligible for military aid. Communist countries are not even considered because of both national security and human rights objections (the one exception being Yugoslavia, which gets assistance to help deter a possible Soviet invasion).

The real issue is what circumstances justify military aid to a government engaged in harsh repression of its own people. The Reagan criticism implies that it is enough if the government in question is "friendly" to us. But if no compelling interest of ours is at stake, how can it be morally or politically sound to aid forces that may torture, kill, and imprison innocent people?

4) *The human rights policy destabilized the shah in Iran and Somoza in Nicaragua. If we had only supported those friends they would have remained in power.* The shah and Somoza were victims of profound social and political revolutions that were decades in the making. To say that the human rights policy was responsible for their downfall is to ignore Montesquieu's maxim that "great events have great causes."

And would someone please explain with specifics, instead of with rhetoric, how to save a regime when its people have turned against it? Do the human rights critics advocate the

Soviet model of massive armed intervention and brutal repression, as in Afghanistan? If not, how would they have kept the shah and Somoza from being deposed by mass movements of their own people?

There is much evidence that human rights will be jettisoned in the foreign policy of the Reagan administration: the nomination of Ernest Lefever, an extreme critic of the Carter policy, as assistant secretary of state for human rights; in Secretary of State Haig's statement that "fighting terrorism" would replace human rights as a cornerstone of our diplomacy; and in the decisions to accord a warm welcome to South Korean dictator Chun, to restore some commercial and defense ties with Chile, and to increase military aid to the junta in El Salvador.

But before the Reagan administration consigns the human rights policy to the diplomatic scrap heap, it will have to contend with a pro-human rights bipartisan coalition on the House Foreign Affairs Committee. Human rights was the policy of Congress long before Carter's election. Starting in 1973, the House committee initiated human rights legislation which established the State Department bureau, required the submission of annual reports on conditions worldwide, and made the policy a major factor in decisions on economic and military aid.

This committee voted to reverse Carter administration actions that it felt violated the congressional human rights norms. During the last four years, it eliminated proposed military aid to Guatemala and cut back on the amounts sought for the Philippines and Zaire. It also closely monitored Soviet violations of the human rights provisions of the Helsinki Accords.

Just a few weeks ago, the Democratic majority on the committee elected activist pro-human rights members to chair three subcommittees dealing with the third world: Harold Wolpe of Michigan for Africa, Stephen Solarz of New York for Asia, and Michael Barnes of Maryland for Latin America. In two instances they were chosen over colleagues who had more seniority but who wanted to downplay human rights.

The committee can be expected to examine skeptically Reagan proposals for military aid to repressive governments. It may also conduct hearings on the long-run dangers to our national security created by unequivocal support for unpopular regimes. In its role as defender of human rights concerns, it could be as significant a voice in foreign policy under President Reagan as the Fulbright Senate Foreign Relations Committee was during the Vietnam War era.

Because of the House Foreign Affairs Committee, predictions that the human rights policy will disappear may be as overstated as the arguments that it should.

A VICTORY FOR HUMAN RIGHTS[13]

The withdrawal of Ernest Lefever has sent a message to the rest of the world about the United States and its attitude toward human rights. It was the Congress—not the president—that established the Office of Human Rights and Humanitarian Affairs in the State Department. And it was a congressional committee that told a popular president that respect for human rights is still central to the American vision.

The human rights post, to which Lefever was appointed by President Reagan, grew out of a congressional mandate during the Ford administration that United States assistance to other nations had to relate to a standard of human rights consistent with this nation's highest ideals. The post was first filled in 1975, and an annual reporting procedure was established to indicate to the Congress how well these standards

[13] Reprint of editorial comment by James M. Wall. *Christian Century.* 98:691–2. Jl. 1–8, '81. Copyright 1981 Christian Century Foundation. Reprinted by permission from the July 1–8 1981 issue of *The Christian Century.*

were being met. President Carter, who made human rights a
cornerstone of foreign policy, utilized the position to bring
pressure on those nations that were our allies. In today's political climate, that means governments of the right, or those
U.N. Ambassador Jeane J. Kirkpatrick has designated as "authoritarian" rather than "totalitarian."

Under Patt Derian, a former civil rights activist from Mis-
sissippi, the office developed a high profile, and according to
the testimony of many Latin American church leaders, it
helped mitigate the oppressive behavior of such right-wing
regimes as the one in Argentina which has perpetrated well-
documented acts of torture against its opponents.

I

The appointment of Ernest Lefever, therefore, was nothing less than an ill-chosen strategy to signal that the Reagan
administration views the Soviet Union as the pre-eminent
world threat. On strategic grounds, this decision was a mis-
taken one from the outset. The human rights position was established to deal not with our enemies but with our friends,
those nations that receive aid from the U.S.

Backed in the Senate by the strong right-wing clout of
North Carolina Senator Jesse Helms, Lefever seemed nevertheless an inspired choice to carry the banner against the liberals on the issue of human rights. A minister ordained in the
pacifist Church of the Brethren, with a Ph.D. in ethics from
Yale University, Lefever had gained respect within right-
wing circles for his shift from an earlier liberalism to his
present neoconservative posture. He was viewed as an academic who could articulate an anticommunistic stance acceptable to the American public.

His selection outraged the liberal community, which organized quickly with what proved to be an effective coalition
of human rights organizations, church groups and congressional Democrats, hungry for any victory they could find
against a consistently popular conservative president.

The campaign worked. Lefever proved to be both vulnerable and ineffective before the Senate Committee on Foreign Relations. His Ethics and Public Policy Center, consistent with its ideology, had been supportive of the Nestlé Corporation in its fight with liberal critics over the promotion of infant formula for use by Third World mothers. Lefever had also shown greater sympathy for South Africa than U.S. blacks and liberal activists could tolerate. Yet, with the strong backing of President Reagan, he might have survived the Senate hearing had he not been caught in such contradictory testimony that committee chairman Charles Percy had finally to accuse him directly of lying.

Faced with a bitter floor fight which Senator Howard Baker warned the White House it could lose, Lefever withdrew his name from the nomination after the Senate committee voted against him. The liberal coalition had prevailed.

II

But the victory should not be an occasion for gloating. It was a political victory, not an ideological one. Nothing has happened to change the Reagan administration's basic position that the real enemy of the free world is Soviet-style communism. It may also have been a costly victory for the church groups that participated in bringing Lefever down. The identification of liberal Protestantism, including the National Council of Churches, with a political victory underscores the argument of conservative church members that Jerry Falwell's entry into an alliance with right-wing politicians is no different from the kind of alignment formed between liberal politicians and church leaders in the anti-Lefever fight.

In the course of the battle, Lefever learned that politics is not as loving as a Sunday school picnic. He is not a heartless man, nor does he lack compassion. Rather he has a perspective on world politics different from that of his liberal opponents. He holds the currently popular neoconservative view that maintains, as he puts it, that liberals in the past two decades have neglected or trivialized "the fundamental political and moral struggle of our time: the protracted conflict between the forces of total government based on coercion (the left) and the proponents of limited government based on popular consent and humane laws (the right)."

Lefever thought his case was unassailable. Certainly in his own writings, and in those of Ambassador Kirkpatrick, a more thoughtful argument has been made that it is time to be nicer to our friends than to our enemies. But there was a fatal flaw to the presentation that Lefever made to the committee—a problem inherent in any rigid political position, right or left. As George Weigel put it in a recent column in the *Seattle Weekly*, the flaw in Lefever's position was not in "its underlying morality (which seems to me to be impeccable; anyone who doesn't understand the moral difference between the Philippines and Kampuchea is not worth listening to when the topic turns to human rights); the flaw was in its logic." The only policy conclusion that could be drawn from Lefever's authoritarian-versus-totalitarian argument, Weigel writes, "is that the U.S. has to accept lesser evils in order to battle the greater evil." It is simply false logic to say that we must tolerate Argentinas in order to strengthen our hand against Soviet Russia.

In his own writings, Lefever would not be caught in such a simplistic conclusion, but in the heat of the Senate hearings he could not translate his academic nuances into political certainty. He put himself in the position of appearing to oppose the fundamental American principle that the rights of every individual are important. Lefever lacked the political ability to translate what he and Ambassador Kirkpatrick have in mind for U.S. foreign policy into terms acceptable to the general public. The theologian was forced to answer political questions, and he failed the exam.

The battle, however, is now joined. The Congress, through the Semate Committee on Foreign Affairs, has reiterated its commitment to human rights in U.S. foreign policy. If the Reagan administration wants to change that, it will have to present a better case than Lefever did in his unpleasant moments before the Senate committee.

HUMAN RIGHTS AND THE U.S. NATIONAL INTEREST[14]

Few other U.S. foreign policy initiatives have been as misunderstood and as poorly articulated as our human rights policy. The level of debate on this subject has been and continues to be sophomoric, and that is true of the arguments of its proponents and its opponents. Part of the blame rests with President Carter and the fact that he promoted the policy with the righteous rhetoric of a fundamentalist sermon so that much of the discussion of the subject took on a moralistic tone. And the few efforts that were made by the Carter Administration to justify the policy to the public in terms of our national interest did not get much of a hearing.

The current Administration falls into a similar trap. Its spokesmen criticize and reject a strong human rights policy because they see it as having purely moral but very little, if any, political significance. They view it as a propaganda tool to be used against the Soviets, but not to criticize our allies. They argue that totalitarianism of the left is worse than the repression of the right practiced by some of our allies. They contend that the U.S. faces a formidable adversary in Soviet expansionism and cannot afford the luxury of being the moral policeman of the world, imposing its own values on the rest of the world; that the U.S. needs allies and cannot afford to alienate friendly anti-Communist governments even if they are repressive. In short, they contend that what we need is to balance our commitment to human rights against foreign policy assets.

I agree that the Soviet Union and what it stands for presents the most serious threat to the U.S. national interest. But the threat is not only military or subversive, it is also ideological and it must therefore be confronted on the ideological

[14] Reprint of an address by Thomas Buergenthal, Dean of the Washington College of Law of American University, delivered under the sponsorship of the Pan American Development Foundation and Meridian House International. *Vital Speeches of the Day.* 47:414–16. Ap. 15, '81. Reprinted by permission.

level as well. In today's world, ideology is as much a weapon as is sophisticated weaponry. A sound human rights policy provides the U.S. with an ideology that distinguishes us most clearly from the Soviet Union and seriously undercuts the ideological appeal of Communism. It is the only ideology, the only dream, if you will, that the people of the U.S. share with the vast majority of the people of the second and third worlds. The quest for human rights and human dignity is a phenomenon of contemporary life of universal dimensions and immense significance in the struggle between East and West. And those who do not grasp its significance do not know much about the world we live in and the forces that shape it.

All over the world human beings are dying, human beings are being tortured, human beings disappear, are being imprisoned, and are held in insane asylums—all because they believe in the human rights and freedoms the American people take for granted. To suggest that we are imposing our values on others by promoting human rights in other countries, be it against totalitarianism or oppressive regimes, is to reveal one's arrogance and ignorance. If we do not grasp the political and emotional significance of the human rights movement, we shall forfeit the only real competitive advantage we have in the struggle to contain Soviet expansionism and counteract its influence in the developing world.

The human rights policy which the U.S. followed in the past six years—it all started with Congressional action in 1973-4, with President Ford's strong support of the human rights provisions of the Helsinki Final Act, and President Carter's enthusiastic espousal and promotion of human rights—has had a significant impact. In Latin America, for example, it contributed to the establishment of democratic regimes in Peru, Ecuador and, for all too short a period, in Bolivia. It ushered in a liberalization process in a number of other countries in the hemisphere; it led to the entry into force of the American Convention on Human Rights and the establishment of the Inter-American Court of Human Rights. And, most importantly, the U.S. began to lose the image it has had in the hemisphere as a government which allies itself

with and supports oppression in Latin America. The U.S.
began to be seen as a country willing to identify itself with
the aspirations of the people of the region. This realization
opened up democratic alternatives in the hemisphere—one
no longer had to choose only between Communism on the
one hand and rightist oppression on the other.

Please do not misunderstand my emphasis on the political
benefits to the U.S. of a strong human rights policy. I believe
in human rights because I believe it is criminal and immoral
to deny human beings their basic rights and to violate them
with impunity. It doesn't much matter, however, whether
U.S. policymakers share my convictions. If they believe that
morality has no place in foreign policy, so be it. Let them,
therefore, assess the foreign policy benefits of a strong human
rights policy in purely *Realpolitik* terms before they scrap it.

I have already spoken of the comparative advantage we
have in this sphere over the Soviets. If the U.S. wants to exploit this advantage, it has to have an ideologically neutral
human rights policy. By this I mean that it has to express its
opposition to violations of human rights with equal fervor,
whether or not the violations are committed by the left or the
right. The policy to be effective has to be credible and it can
only be credible if it is ideologically neutral. People all around
the world have to see that the U.S. stands for human rights—
not only for human rights in the Soviet Union, but also in
Central America, in South America, in Africa, and in Asia. If
instead we close our eyes to violations by our friends and criticize only our adversaries, we will have reduced the policy to
a mere propaganda tool—and the world will know it for the
hypocrisy it is. And it will not be a foreign policy asset.

All this is not to say that there are no other foreign policy
interests that the U.S. must take into account. Human rights
should not and cannot be the only issue decision-makers have
to take into consideration in shaping foreign policy. It needs
to be treated as an important foreign policy concern, however, and to dismiss it as moral claptrap is to do serious harm
to the U.S. national interest.

A word about intervention which always pops up in discussions about human rights. There is the argument, for example, that it is a violation of international law for one country to compile reports on the state of human rights in another country and to publish these reports. It is also contended that it is illegal intervention for one country to complain publicly that another country is violating human rights. That is nonsense, ladies and gentlemen, both under general international law and under our own hemispheric international law. I don't know of any international lawyer of stature who would seriously espouse that thesis today.

As a political matter, moreover, it is as much intervention for the U.S. today to identify itself with a government that engages in serious violations of human rights as it is to disassociate itself from that government and to take a public stand against those practices. The political reality is that a superpower simply cannot avoid intervention by association; we have to face up to this fact. Given this reality, the only serious issue is whether we are perceived as intervening by identifying ourselves with a repressive regime or by expressing our opposition to repression. I believe it is not in the U.S. national interest to support or be identified with repressive regimes whether of the left or the right.

Those opposing an effective U.S. human rights policy argue that it contributes to the demise of governments friendly to the U.S. In my opinion, this is a simplistic view of the impact of the policy. It is rarely ever a question of the demise or survival of a regime. If a government friendly to the U.S. engages in repressive practices, U.S. policy, if properly managed and articulated, can move the government, over time, either towards more repression or towards less repression. The best example of this phenomenon occurred since the new Administration took over. It was perceived, rightly or wrongly, as opposing human rights, and immediately some governments in the hemisphere began to crack down on human rights activists, not because they had suddenly become a threat to the regime, but because the time was ripe. Most of the once friendly governments lost to the U.S. side were lost because of their long history of repression and our identification with those regimes; they were not lost because of our human rights policy.

Of course, I do not believe that the U.S. should "destabilize" governments, but I believe that it can and should make its influence felt. As a matter of fact, as a superpower, particularly in this hemisphere, it cannot avoid making its influence felt, and the only issue is whether it will opt for a policy that is in the U.S. national interest or detrimental to it.

To conclude, ladies and gentlemen, what worries me most about our current policy direction is that the Administration appears to have decided upon a serious foreign policy change without having thoroughly examined the question whether in fact the U.S. national interest is advanced or harmed by a strong human rights policy. What we have heard thus far on the subject are slogans. What is lacking is substantial evidence and analysis.

I, for one, believe that it would be a serious political blunder for the U.S. to abandon a policy that identifies us with the aspirations of the people of our hemisphere and the world. Given our own political system and traditions, a credible U.S. human rights policy can enjoy the support of the American people, do some good in the world, and advance our national interest. That is why I believe that it needs to be preserved.

BIBLIOGRAPHY

An asterisk (*) preceding a reference indicates that the article or part of it has been reprinted in this book.

BOOKS AND PAMPHLETS

Amnesty International report, 1980. Amnesty International Publications (London). '80.
* Christopher, Warren. Human rights and the national interest. (address before the American Bar Association, August 4, '80) Current Policy No. 206. U.S. Department of State, Bureau of Public Affairs. '80.
Domínguez, J. I. and others. Enhancing global human rights. (1980s Project/ Council on Foreign Relations) McGraw-Hill. '79.
* Educational Broadcasting Corporation. The MacNeil-Lehrer report on human rights. '81.
* Foreign Policy Association. Great decisions '78: human rights abroad—reality or illusion for U.S. policy. '78.
Frankel, Charles. Human rights and foreign policy. (Headline ser., 24) Foreign Policy Association. '78.
Frankel, Charles. Morality and U.S. foreign policy. (Headline ser., no.24) Foreign Policy Association. '75.
Garling, Marguerite, comp. The human rights handbook; a guide to British and American international human rights organizations. Facts on File. '79.
Haas, E. B. Global evangelism rides again; how to protect human rights without really trying. University of California Institute of International Studies. '78.
The International Bill of Rights, Universal Declaration of Human Rights, United Nations Office of Public Information. '78.
Kommers, D. P. and Loescher, Gilburt, eds. Human rights and American foreign policy. University of Notre Dame Press. '79.
Timerman, Jacobo. Prisoner without a name, cell without a number. Knopf. '81.
Vogelgesang, Sandy. American dream, global nightmare; the dilemma of U.S. human rights policy. Norton. '80.
Woito, Robert, ed. International human rights kit. World Without War Council. '77.

PERIODICALS

America. 144:59–61. Ja. 24 '81. Toleration, Soviet style. Walter
    Parchomenko.
America. 144:inside cover. F. 14 '81. Of many things [Alexander
    Haig's statement on human rights and foreign policy]. J. A.
    O'Hare.
° America. 144:220–1. Mr. 21 '81. Firm resistance on human
    rights.
American Journal of International Law. 75:169–72. Ja. '81. Appli-
    cation of the International covenant on civil and political
    rights in New Zealand. J. B. Elkind.
American Political Science Review. 73:781–94; 74:783–4. S. '79; S.
    '80. Alternative conceptualization of political tolerance: illu-
    sory increases 1950s–1970s. J. L. Sullivan and others.
Bulletin of the Atomic Scientists. 37:5. Mr. '81. Carter's legacy
    [nuclear arms control, environmental degradation and human
    rights]. B. T. Feld.
Christian Century. 98:49–51. Ja. 21 '81. Brazil: new hopes and old
    fears. J. K. Black.
Christian Century. 98:187–8. F. 25 '81. From Derian to Lefever
    [appointment as head of State Department's Office for
    Human Rights]. J. M. Wall.
Christian Century. 98:205–6. F. 25 '81. Playing hardball with
    human rights. W. R. Phillippe.
Christian Century. 98:226–9. Mr. 4 '81. Jeane Kirkpatrick: utilitar-
    ianism as U.S. foreign policy. M. D. Wilde.
Christian Century. 98:252–3. Mr. 11 '81. Playing favorites among
    terrorists. Dean Peerman.
° Christian Century. 98:691–2. Jl. 1–8 '81. Victory for human
    rights [rejection of E. W. Lefever's nomination to office of
    Human Rights]. J. M. Wall.
Christianity and Crisis. 41:36–45. Mr. 2 '81. Ernest Lefever at the
    edge of power: a profile in consistency. Leon Howell.
Commentary. 71:29–40. Ja. '81. U. S. security & Latin America.
    Jeane Kirkpatrick.
Commonweal. 108:69–70. F. 13 '81. Terrorism & rights [Alexander
    Haig's statement on human rights and foreign policy].
Comparative Politics. 13:149–70. Ja. '81. U.S. foreign policy and
    human rights violations in Latin America: a comparative
    analysis of foreign aid distributions. Lars Schoultz.
Current History. 80:149–53+. Ap. '81. Opposition movement in
    Poland. R. F. Staar.

Current History. 80:154–8+. Ap. '81. Czechoslovakia and the Polish virus. Otto Ulč.

Education Digest. 46:21–4. F. '81. U.S. Supreme Court decisions on diversity. C. E. Cortés and V. L. Perkins.

Encounter. 55:53–6+. D. '80. Coming of Leviathan; human rights. Ferdinand Mount.

Foreign Affairs. 58:775–96. Spring '80. Human rights and foreign policy: a proposal. W. F. Buckley, Jr.

* Freedom at Issue. p 2. Ja.-F. '81. Freedom in the world—1981.

Freedom at Issue. p 3–19. Ja.-F. '81. Comparative survey of freedom—the ninth year. R. D. Gastil.

International Affairs. 56:579–606. Autumn '80. Human rights and foreign policy. Evan Luard.

Journal of Modern African Studies. 18 no3:509–24. '80. Retreat into the future: the United States, South Africa, and human rights, 1976–8. Christopher Coker.

Law and Contemporary Problems. 43:66–82. Summer '80. Recrudescence of property rights as the foremost principle of civil liberties: the first decade of the Burger court. W. W. Van Alstyne.

* Maclean's. 93:25–30. N. 24 '80. Global struggle for human rights. Marci McDonald.

Maclean's. 93:27. N. 24 '80. A tug-of-war in Madrid. David Baird.

Maclean's. 93:29. N. 24 '80. Some rooms to clean at home.

Maclean's. 93:22–4. D. 8 '80. Two rights may make a wrong. John Hay.

Maclean's. 94:23. Ja. 26 '81. Little bat, a little blood. Susan Riley.

Maclean's. 94:34. Mr. 16 '81. White House turns a blind eye. Robert Cox.

Maclean's. 94:61. My. 4 '81. Right to be bullied and bored. Barbara Amiel.

Monist. 63:135–55. Ap. '80. Right to life. G. P. Fletcher.

Nation. 232:195–6. F. 21 '81. Worst Yet [appointment of E. W. Lefever as Assistant Secretary of State for Human Rights and Humanitarian Affairs].

Nation. 232:323–4. Mr. 21 '81. Cheer for Pat [D. P. Moynihan].

Nation. 232:361–4. Mr. 28 '81. Kirkpatrick doctrine for Latin America. Penny Lernoux.

* National Review. 33:364+. Ap. 3 '81. Real case for human rights. Michael Novak.

* National Review. 33:494. My. 1 '81. Winter before spring. Michael Novak.

* National Review. 33:688–9. Je. 12 '81. Kirkpatrick's four distinctions. W. F. Buckley, Jr.

National Review. 33:689. Je. 12 '81. Jews in Argentina. W. F. Buckley, Jr.

* Nation's Business. 68:52. O. '80. Wrongs of the rights policy.

New Leader. 64:7–10. Ja. 12 '81. Foreign policy in a bipolar world. G. P. Brockway.

New Leader. 64:6–7. F. 9 '81. Rattling the Russians in Madrid. William Korey.

New Republic. 184:7. F. 14 '81. Mixed signals [Reagan administration's position].

* New Republic. 184:13–14. Mr. 28 '81. Wrong on human rights. Stephen Cohen.

* New Republic. 184:16–21. Je. 27 '81. Siege of the Argentine Jews. Robert Weisbrot.

* New Republic. 184:18–19. Je. 27 '81. Kristol unclear. John Lieber.

New York Review of Books. 28:44–5. Je. 11 '81. Appeal in Iran.

* New York Times. A10. F. 10 '81. U.S. report says status of rights improved during '80.

New York Times. A10. Jl. 15 '81. Haig aide insists U.S. rights policy is evenhanded.

New York University Journal of International Law and Politics. 13:427–72. Winter '81. Political sources of procedural debates in the United Nations: structural impediments to implementation of human rights. T. D. Gonzales.

* New Yorker. 56:31–2. F. 16 '81. Notes and comment.

Newsweek. 97:61. F. 9 '81. Deng takes one step back. Melinda Liu.

* Newsweek. 97:47. Mr. 16 '81. Crackdown on rights [case of E. Mignone]. John Brecher.

Newsweek. 97:18+. My. 18 '81. Peace Prize winner: 'now people listen' [work of A. Pérez Esquivel]. Eileen Keerdoja and Larry Rohter.

Philosophy and Public Affairs. 9:372–84. Summer '80. Two concepts of rights. Phillip Montague.

Progressive. 45:28–31. Mr. '81. Welcome to Peking . . . where some are more equal than others. Ron Dorfman.

Senior Scholastic. 113:2, 14–17. Ja. 9 '81. Prisoners of conscience. Douglas Reichert.

Social Theory and Practice. 5 no.3–4:427–59. '79. General theory of rights. D. W. Haslett.

Social Theory and Practice. 5 no.3–4:461–88. '79. Human rights and moral ideals: an essay on the moral theory of liberalism. D. A. J. Richards.

Today's Education. 70:15GS-17GS. Ap./ My. '81. Human rights: an international perspective: What can teachers do to protect human rights? Motofumi Makieda.

UN Chronicle. 17:39–40. Jl. '80. Committee concludes that Uruguay violated human rights covenant.

UN Chronicle. 17:63–6. S./ O. '80. Committee considers reports on human rights situation in four countries.

UN Chronicle. 18:42–4. F. '81. Assembly states concern at human rights situations in El Salvador, Chile; acts on Bolivia question.

UN Chronicle. 18:49–50. F. '81. Human Rights Day marked; calls issued for continued UN efforts.

UN Chronicle. 18:57. Mr. '81. Call for continued work on measures to protect rights of migrant workers.

UN Chronicle. 18:58. Mr. '81. Study of extension of mandate of Chile Trust Fund urged.

UN Chronicle. 18:58–9. Mr. '81. Experts urge study on legitimacy of South Africa government.

UN Chronicle. 18:41–7. Je. '81. Committee, in productive session, examines human rights situation in four countries.

UNESCO Courier. 33:5–9. S. '80. Education, disarmament and human rights. Judith Torney and Leonard Gambrell.

U.S. Department of State Bulletin. 81:18–20. Ja. '81. Strengthening the CSCE process. G. B. Bell.

* U.S. Department of State Bulletin. 81:21–3. Ja. '81. Human rights and international law. P. M. Derian.

* U.S. Department of State Bulletin. 81:54. F. '81. Bill of Rights Day, Human Rights Day and Week, 1980. Jimmy Carter.

* U.S. Department of State, Publication 8959: Human rights and U.S. foreign policy. Office of Public Communications, Bureau of Public Affairs. D. '78.

U.S. News & World Report. 85:32–3. D. 4 '78. Only 1 in 3 around the world lives in freedom.

U.S. News & World Report. 90:37–8. F. 9 '81. Russia's record since Helsinki: 5 years of cheating. M. M. Kampelman.

U.S. News & World Report. 90:9. F. 23 '81. Human rights: better, but still battered.

* U.S. News & World Report. 90:49–50. Mr. 2 '81. Overhaul U.S. policy on human rights? [interviews] Jeane Kirkpatrick; P. M. Derian.

Vital Speeches of the Day. 47:242–6. F. 1 '81. Equality faces a dangerous decade. R. Y. Woodhouse.

* Vital Speeches of the Day. 47:414–16. Ap. 15 '81. Human rights and the U.S. national interest. Thomas Buergenthal.

Wall Street Journal. 197:34. Mr. 24 '81. What is proper human
    rights policy? Ferdinand Mount.
* Wall Street Journal. 197:28. Ap. 8 '81. The common sense of
    human rights. Irving Kristol.
Wall Street Journal. 197:30. Ap. 28 '81. The Reagan approach to
    human rights. Michael Novak.
Wall Street Journal. 197:32. Je. 9 '81. The human rights office was
    a poor idea: elevating human rights to the status of a bureau
    of the State Department, headed by an assistant secretary,
    was a mistake.
World Affairs. 143:226–63. Winter '80/ '81. Speeches by the
    U.S. delegation before the United Nations Commission on
    Human Rights. Michael Novak and Richard Schifter.
* World Today. 37:63–8. F. '81. Human rights in Latin America—
    a watershed? Edy Kaufman.

DATE DUE

date
due